You Can Be
A Soulwinner

You Can Be A Soulwinner

by
Norvel Hayes

HARRISON HOUSE
Tulsa, Oklahoma

Unless otherwise indicated,
all Scripture quotations are taken from
the *King James Version* of the Bible.

3rd Printing
Over 22,500 in Print

You Can Be A Soulwinner
ISBN 0-89274-269-0
Copyright © 1983 by Norvel Hayes
P. O. Box 1379
Cleveland, Tennessee 37311

Published by Harrison House, Inc.
P. O. Box 35035
Tulsa, Oklahoma 74153

Printed in the United States of America.
All rights reserved under International Copyright Law.
Contents and/or cover may not be reproduced in whole or
in part in any form without the express written consent
of the Publisher.

Contents

Introduction 7
1 Jesus Came to Save 13
2 The Faithful Witness 33
3 Ordained to Witness 53
4 Witnessing With Authority 67
5 Witnessing in Love 77
6 Pay the Price for Power 95
7 Practical Suggestions for Effective Witnessing 117
8 Questions and Answers on Effective Witnessing 133

Introduction

In this book I want to inspire you to be a soulwinner, to get people to believe in Jesus. People believe in all kinds of things. Some believe in their church or pastor or denomination. Some believe what their parents or grandparents believed. But none of that is going to help them. Some don't know what they believe. A person must come to the place where he believes in Jesus Christ, because He is the life-giver—there is no other.

You must share Jesus with others if they are to come to know Him personally. You have to do it in love and understanding and compassion. If you don't zero in on people and get them to confess Jesus as Lord and Savior, then your efforts are wasted. Their church will give them tradition. But tradition has never saved anyone. In fact, it has kept many people out of the Kingdom of God.

That is one reason many Christians lose their anointing and lose the power of God. They get involved in other things besides sharing Jesus Christ. Sometimes Full Gospel churches get so caught up in activity—praising God and shouting and singing and dancing—that if they don't have a "high time" in their service they think they haven't done anything. Many churches are so wrapped up in "high services" they don't have any kind of soulwinning program. If that goes on for two or three years, that church will eventually wind up half dead. It will dry up. Such churches have to continually work themselves up with something, using whatever program or activity they've been used to.

But I'll guarantee you that if you will make it a practice to win souls for God, the sweet, tender compassion of the Lord will boil up out of your spirit like a spray of water—a well of water springing up out of your innermost being. It will be precious to you all the time. Your Christian walk can be precious to you every day. It will never get stale. I don't have any sad days or beaten-down days. All my days with Jesus are precious. They're all supposed to be that way.

But in order for that to happen to you, you have to give out what the Lord has given you. Don't just get caught up in having "high services." That kind of spiritual "high" is good in its place, but sometimes you need to get still and know that God is God. You have to share the Lord with others. When you do, it keeps your spirit tender before the Lord. If you don't, you get hard. Your mind and heart become hardened, and it won't be long until you are led astray by familiar spirits.

I lived for eight years in Indianapolis, Indiana, not far from a church which was pastored by Jim Jones, the man who later led a cult following to

Guyana, South America. Since I belonged to the First Baptist Church then, I never did go to his church; but I'm sure that at that time he was all right. Most of those fellows were all right at one time or another. They loved the Lord. But by degrees they were led off into error. Why? One reason was because they didn't give out what they received; they didn't pass on to others what the Lord was giving them. Without a soulwinning program, without an outreach to others, you become unbalanced. Familiar spirits start to take over. Not all of a sudden, just little by little.

You have to watch yourself in the work of the Lord so that you try not to have your own thing. I don't care how powerful you get, you can't have your own thing. You have to have God's thing going. And God's thing is Jesus.

From the time you get up in the morning till you go to bed at night, it's either Jesus or nothing. Either you have His love and compassion and His vision for the lost and dying, or you don't. Either you put Him first, or you put self first. If it's self first, then you're going to get messed up.

Without a vision, the Bible says, the people perish. (Prov. 29:18.) So don't ever lose your vision. If you ever get to the point where you don't care about winning souls, where you don't want to testify for Jesus or help those who are beaten down, then you had better get down on your knees right then and pray—one hour, two hours, three hours, however long it takes—until that compassion comes back to you. If you don't, I'm warning you, you'll end up living in a world of spiritual darkness.

There are all kinds of spirits out there, and they will try to rob you of the blessing of God and make you cold. They don't want you to win souls. But God wants you to be a soulwinner. I don't care if He has made you the best teacher or pastor in the world. It doesn't matter if you're worth ten million dollars, Jesus still wants you to be a soulwinner. He never wants you to get so busy that you can't sit down with someone and tell them about Him; or go to someone's house who is in need and minister to him. God wants you to demonstrate the same kind of love and compassion that Jesus demonstrated.

When people would drive Jesus out of one town, He would say to His disciples, "Let's just leave this town and go to another." That is what we've been called to do. That's what we're here for—to go from town to town and place to place to bring the good news of what God has done for them in Christ Jesus. Jesus wouldn't quit; neither should we. I don't care how people treat you, there is no quitting, no turning back. Remember that. It doesn't matter whether they accept your testimony or not; it doesn't change your responsibility at all.

In the third chapter of John, we read these words:

> *He that cometh from above is above all: he that is of the earth is earthly, and speaketh of the earth: he that cometh from heaven is above all.*
>
> *John 3:31*

When you go out to witness to others about Jesus, remember this fact. Get it firmly settled in your spirit, once and for all: The One you're talking about is above everything. Jesus Christ is above all. It doesn't matter how many people you meet or how strong their personality might be; the One you are representing is above them. Jesus is above all.

And what he hath seen and heard, that he testifieth; and no man receiveth his testimony.

He that hath received his testimony hath set to his seal that God is true.

For he whom God hath sent speaketh the words of God: for God giveth not the Spirit by measure unto him.

The Father loveth the Son, and hath given all things into his hand.

He that believeth on the Son hath everlasting life: and he that believeth not the Son shall not see life; but the wrath of God abideth on him.
John 3:32-36

If a person does not believe on the Son, he is lost. It is just that simple. That is our reason for witnessing. As the Apostle Paul asks:

How then shall they call on him in whom they have not believed? and how shall they believe in him of whom they have not heard? and how shall they hear without a preacher?
Romans 10:14

If you have accepted Jesus Christ as your Lord and Savior, you are that preacher—you are called to share Jesus with others so that they too might believe and be saved.

And you are not called to do something you are not capable of doing. If you will learn who you are in Christ Jesus, the angels of God can work for you. Stand up for your rights in Christ. You don't have to take fear or defeat of any kind from anyone, human being or devil.

Make this commitment right now. Say:

I am the head and not the tail. I have victory and not defeat. I am well and not sick. I am strong and not weak. I am a soulwinner. I will testify for Jesus. I will tell people what Jesus has done for me. It will be the greatest sermon I could ever preach, because Jesus is above all.

Now just remember that. Remember that Jesus is above all. And He is with you as you go. Because of who you are in Him, you can be an effective witness for Him.

1
Jesus Came to Save

Jesus came for one reason: to save. He did not come to the earth just to be beaten with those stripes in order to pay the price for healing. Of course, healing is involved in salvation. Salvation in its fullest sense covers all of our needs—physical, mental, emotional, financial, material, social, and spiritual. But basically Jesus came to die on the cross of Calvary so that the world might be born again and saved.

God saw that man could never save himself. It is impossible for a man to go to heaven in a physical body. He has to have his spirit reborn. He must take on the nature of God on the inside and he must keep that spirit on the inside stronger than the one on the outside, stronger than the house of flesh he lives in. If he doesn't, he will wind up in hell. The ways of the world, the ways of the flesh, the ways of the devil will take him to hell.

But if a person will get his spirit reborn by the Spirit of God, and then study God's Word and take orders from the Holy Ghost Who lives inside him, he can go to heaven and live there for all eternity. He can also take a lot of other people with him.

If you don't keep your spirit built up, you may go to heaven, but you won't take anyone with you. Without that strong spirit within you, you will just go to church on Sunday morning and maybe on Sunday evening and hardly ever on Wednesday night, but you are not going to take anybody to heaven with you because you are not strong enough. You can't be a weakling and take folks to heaven with you.

You can't go into people's homes and bring them help unless you are strong. You can't set free those who are possessed of demons unless you are more powerful than those demons. You have to have a solid foundation built up in your spirit to be able to say, "Devil, come out, in the name of Jesus Christ! I command you to let this person go free!" To break the power of the devil over a human life, you must be strong in the spirit. Once you know who you are in Jesus Christ, you can do that.

You can break the power of cancer in your own body, if you know how to do it. It's very simple. All you have to do is say, "In Jesus' name, cancer, I break your power—you can't stay in me! I curse you, cancer. I command you to die, in Jesus' name. Get out of my body!" If you will do that and keep on doing it for a few hours, that cancer will come out of you. Don't let anyone tell you it won't because I know it will. Of course, you can't do that if you don't know how.

You can be set free from anything, no matter what it is. You can be free from any devil, any disease, any weakness. You don't have to be weak. You can be strong. But there is a price you must pay to develop that kind of spiritual power.

One of the reasons I don't give up and let myself get weak is because I keep myself in the love of God. I keep myself in God's holy presence enough so that I won't get so weak that I fall by the wayside and have my Christian walk become dull. This walk never gets dull to me. I don't have weak days, or bad days, or "blue Mondays." All my days are strong! God doesn't believe in "blue Mondays." He doesn't have any, so why should I?

You can't afford "off days." You have to stay ready to witness to people. Remember, Jesus came to save, and He left you with the task of sharing that salvation with others.

You might say, "Well, Jesus can save people without my help." No, He can't. He has to have you.

Sent by God

There was a man of the Pharisees, named Nicodemus, a ruler of the Jews:

The same came to Jesus by night, and said unto him, Rabbi, we know that thou art a teacher come from God . . . .
John 3:1,2

That's what you are—a teacher sent from God. In Matthew 28:19,20 Jesus commanded His disciples:

Go ye therefore, and teach all nations, baptizing them in the name of the Father, and of the Son, and of the Holy Ghost:

> *Teaching them to observe all things whatsoever I have commanded you: and, lo, I am with you alway, even unto the end of the world.*

That's what you and I are to do—teach. Now the devil surely doesn't do that. That's our job, our calling, our commission. We are teachers sent from God.

You Must Be Born Again

> *. . . for no man can do these miracles that thou doest, except God be with him.*
>
> *Jesus answered and said unto him, Verily, verily, I say unto thee, Except a man be born again, he cannot see the kingdom of God.*
>
> *Marvel not that I said unto thee, Ye must be born again.*
>
> John 3:2,3,7

"You must be born again. You must be born again to go to heaven." Get yourself in the habit of saying these words so when you come upon a sinner they won't sound so strange to you, so you can say to them with love and compassion and without embarrassment: "You must be born again." Never be ashamed to ask people if they are born again—if they know that they know that they know it.

We sometimes assume that if a person is a member of a church, then he is born again. But that is just not so. Many church members are not born again. A good test to determine if a person is born again is just to ask him if he is. If he can't tell you with absolute certainty that he is born again, that is strong evidence that he is not.

You can't be born again and not know it. When the Spirit of God comes in and changes the nature of your spirit from the inside, you know He's in there. Brother, you know it. If you don't know that He is in there, He's not. It's just that simple.

If the Spirit of God is in your heart, then you will be moved to share Jesus with others. If you have not been doing that, it's time to begin. Jesus came to save, and those He has saved He has commissioned to carry salvation to others. If you are born again of the Spirit of God, you are sent of God.

Power for Witnessing

Now you may be thinking, *But I can't witness for Jesus. I can't cast out devils. I can't set people free. I don't have the power.*

But I'm telling you that you can do it. God's power is available to you to save people or heal them or to do anything else that needs to be done for them. God's power is available. But to avail yourself of that power you have to have the love of God.

The love of God is the strongest witnessing tool you could ever hope to have. If you can't have compassion on a person who is lost and beaten down, then you are no use to God. If you're not willing to put your arms around people in need, whatever that need might be, and witness to them as the Holy Spirit directs, then you might as well stay home. When you go out to witness to people, you have to become a part of them and get involved in their particular situation, whatever it may be.

Let the Holy Spirit lead and direct you. He'll show you what to do. He might tell you to go over and put your arms around a person. Whatever He tells you to do to minister to the needs of others, do it. That's where the power for witnessing comes from—just following the leading of the Holy Spirit.

I have been in people's homes and had them tell me, "No, you can't pray for me. I don't want that kind of stuff here." So I would just keep on talking to them for a few minutes to give them one last chance for the Spirit of the Lord to touch their heart. I've looked them in the face and said, "Mister, it won't hurt to pray for your family. It doesn't make any difference what you believe—I can't help that. But would you let me pray for your family? It won't hurt to ask God to bless them."

You see, I know that in desperate cases like this, if I walk out the door, that family will probably go to hell because the man has run off the last four or five people who have come to witness to them. I have learned that if I can ever get a person like this to show enough respect for God to bow his head and close his eyes, then I can use the power of prayer to break down that wall of resistance.

But when I pray in these cases, I don't pray a short prayer. If I do, it will all be over. I get the person to bow his head before God and just start praying. Once I start to pray, I don't stop. I pray for five or ten or fifteen minutes. As I pray, I listen to the Holy

Ghost. I say out loud: "Oh, God, I know You love this man. You made this man, Lord, and I know You love him. You love him as much as anybody in the world." I just start telling that man how much God loves him, and it usually won't be very long before I can feel the Holy Ghost moving up inside me. I can feel the presence of God start sweeping through the house. In a little while I will look up at the man and tears will be streaming down his face. He'll be standing there shaking. I tell you, friend, the Holy Ghost shakes people who need to be shaken; and hardened people like that need to be shaken by the power of the Holy Ghost. **The love of God is the strongest tool for witnessing.**

You're Not Alone

When you start to witness to somebody, it is important that you remember one thing: You're not alone. Keep reminding yourself: "I'm not alone when I witness for Jesus." Never let the spirit of fear overtake you and talk you out of witnessing for the Lord. It will do so if you allow it to. The spirit of fear is strong in this world. Just stand firm and rebuke that spirit.

Say, "Spirit of fear, I break your power, in Jesus' name. I command you to go from me. I'm not afraid to knock on the door. I'm not afraid to witness for Jesus. Stop buffeting me, you foul spirit of fear. Leave me alone! I'm not weak; I'm strong in the Lord."

You **can** witness for Jesus. You **do** have the ability and the power. You just have to know what the Lord has sent you to do, and then do it. When you go out to witness, listen to what the Spirit of God says to you. The Holy Ghost will give you the words you need. You will know what to do. You're not alone.

The Mind of the Spirit

That which is born of the flesh is flesh; and that which is born of the Spirit is spirit.
John 3:6

You are not supposed to think opposite from the Spirit. When you lose your vision of winning lost souls for God, then you are no longer thinking like the Holy Spirit—you're thinking like yourself. You have left your calling. You have left what God has given you to do and have started doing your own thing. You can't do that.

That which is born of the Spirit is spirit. You are supposed to have the same kind of vision that the Holy Spirit has, the same kind of compassion and faithfulness that the Lord Jesus Christ Himself had, because you have the same Spirit in you that He had in Him. If Jesus had that kind of dedication to the Gospel, so can you.

For me there is no return, because I've already made my commitment. There are no detours; I've already made up my mind. I want the same Spirit that flowed from Jesus to flow through me.

Now I know that I am not as yielded a vessel as Jesus was, but I can be a part of His ministry. I may not be able to accomplish all that Jesus accomplished,

Jesus Came to Save

but I can do what God wants me to do. I can't do it all perhaps, but I am determined to do all that I can.

Any Christian can do the things Jesus did if he is willing to pay the price that Jesus did. But that's the problem. Most Christians are not willing to pay that price.

Jesus would spend all night long in prayer. Most Christians can't make it through a Sunday morning church service without dozing off.

Jesus fasted forty days and nights. When was the last time you did that?

You see, God will give you as much power as you can stand, as much as you are willing to pay the price for. God can't bless a lazy Christian. In order to be used of God, you must pay the price. One part of that price is to have the mind of the Spirit. You have to keep thinking like God thinks.

We are just now beginning to see God manifesting Himself as He really wants to do. The Church of Jesus Christ is going to see God manifest Himself in the future like we've never heard of before. But we have to get ready for it. The reason God doesn't manifest Himself more than He does now is because we haven't been ready for it. But in the past few years God has been raising up some churches which are not ashamed to praise and worship Him. And God manifests Himself in praise and worship.

God doesn't usually manifest Himself too well through programs. He just lets people do their own thing. The result is that there are many beautiful church buildings filled with beautiful people holding beautiful church services, but there is little real power, little manifestation of God's mighty saving and healing power. **God is not the God of programs; He is the God of people.** These churches become so programmed, so organized, so managed that they never really open up to worship and praise God. Consequently, they never experience any real manifestation of the power and presence of the Lord.

The Bible says to lift up holy hands to God. (1 Tim. 2:8.) "Well, we're not going to do that," some churches say. "We're going to sing three songs, have a sermon, and that's it." Such churches may have excellent sermons and soulwinning programs; but if they are not free to worship and praise God, they will not have the power they need to meet the needs of those Satan has been devouring. God manifests His power where there is praise and worship and faith. Without these, there just isn't enough power there for cripples to rise up and walk or for blind eyes or deaf ears to be opened.

Some churches will not lay hands on the sick. They say, "We just don't do that here." But laying on of hands is not man's idea; it is a directive from God. It is a doctrine of the Church of Jesus Christ. It's not optional; it's something that every church is supposed to do.

In the Great Commission Jesus said:

> *And these signs shall follow them that believe; In my name shall they cast out devils; they shall speak with new tongues;*

Jesus Came to Save

> *. . . they shall lay hands on the sick, and they shall recover.*
>
> Mark 16:17,18

According to this passage, any church which does not cast out devils or lay hands on the sick is out of God's will.

If we, as the Body of Christ, want the power of God manifested in our churches as it was in the New Testament days, then we are going to have to do what God has specifically told us to do. We must stick to the Bible if we want God to manifest Himself in power.

And the same goes for you and me as individuals. If we want to see God manifest Himself in power in our lives, then we must also follow the example set by the first disciples: *And they went forth, and preached every where, the Lord working with them, and confirming the word with signs following* (Mark 16:20).

Those people who are born of the Spirit are spirit. When you go out to witness, remember what you are. You are born of the Spirit. Don't let the natural part of you say, "Well, I don't know if I can do this or not. This might be too hard. I'm just little ol' me." No! That's **not** who you are. If you are born again of the Spirit, you are spirit.

Say to yourself, *The Holy Spirit of God is in me. I have a right to think like God thinks.* When you begin to think like God thinks, people will get set free, because you are not alone. God will work with you to confirm His Word with signs following.

Led of the Spirit

Marvel not that I said unto thee, Ye must be born again.

The wind bloweth where it listeth, and thou hearest the sound thereof, but canst not tell whence it cometh, and whither it goeth: so is every one that is born of the Spirit.
John 3:7,8

That's the way it is with me when I am ministering—I never know what's going to happen next. Whatever the Holy Spirit tells me to do, I do. When you are born of the Spirit, when you are Spirit-filled and Spirit-led, it is exciting! You never know what you are going to do next. You live and move and have your being in Him. (Acts 17:28.) Each new day, every new experience brings something different. The Spirit-led life is never dull. It's always exciting!

When you are born of the Spirit of God, you are not your own any longer. You are His instrument to be used of Him. You allow Him to guide and direct you, to live and act through you. The result is the most fulfilling, adventurous, exciting, and satisfying life you can ever imagine.

Not All Will Receive

Nicodemus answered and said unto him, How can these things be?

Jesus answered and said unto him, Art thou a master of Israel, and knowest not these things?

Jesus Came to Save

> *Verily, verily, I say unto thee, We speak that we do know, and testify that we have seen; and ye receive not our witness.*
>
> John 3:9-11

Be warned. When you go out to witness, there will always be those who will not receive your witness. Be prepared for that. Many will receive, and it will be a great joy and blessing to you. But you must also know that some will not receive. That's where the love of God comes in.

Don't argue about the Bible. **If you want to win a person to God, don't argue.** The love of God is the strongest tool you'll ever have to witness. If God's love can't reach people, you can never hope to do it by arguing with them. God has plainly told us not to argue about His Word. It has already been spoken from the mouth of God. It has already been written, and that's the way it is. People will either accept it or reject it. Your job is not to convince them with arguments, but to witness to them with love. You are not there to argue, but to witness to the truth. Know the Bible, know the truth, because the truth will set you (and them) free. (John 8:32.)

There will always be those who refuse the truth. Don't let that disturb you or discourage you. Just remember, some people even refused to accept the testimony of Jesus Himself.

Lift Up Jesus

> *If I have told you earthly things, and ye believe not, how shall ye believe, if I tell you of heavenly things?*

And no man hath ascended up to heaven, but he that came down from heaven, even the Son of man which is in heaven.

And as Moses lifted up the serpent in the wilderness, even so must the Son of man be lifted up:

That whosoever believeth in him should not perish, but have eternal life.
John 3:12-15

Your job in witnessing to others is to lift up Jesus. If you lift Him up, you'll find that great things will happen. Tell people that Jesus loves them. The world out there doesn't know that Jesus loves them. They have no earthly idea what we are talking about. But they need to know. That's why we are sent—to tell them.

But before you go out to tell others about Jesus, you need to pray. You need to spend time every day praying in the Spirit, but you absolutely must pray before going out to witness. If you don't, I can tell you what will happen. The first time someone gets nasty and slams the door in your face or threatens to call the police if you don't leave, the devil is going to convince you right quick that you're not called to a witnessing ministry—that yours is a prayer ministry!

But that's not true! You have a witnessing ministry. You might have a prayer ministry, too, but everybody is supposed to be a witness. You ought to get it out of your head once and for all that witnessing is not your ministry. You see, the devil told you that. Did you ever say, ''Witnessing—knocking on doors

Jesus Came to Save

and winning families to God and bringing sinners to church—that's some people's ministry, but it's not mine"? That's a lie straight from hell! Don't buy it. The devil told you that, not God.

There should never be empty seats in your church. They should all be full of sinners.

"Full of sinners? You mean I'm supposed to bring a sinner to church with me?"

Absolutely. When was the last time you brought one? That's what you're out there for! You are a soulwinner, whether you know it or not, whether you accept it or not. It's your job to win souls. The question isn't: "Is soulwinning my ministry?" It's your ministry all right. There's no doubt about that. The question is: "Am I fulfilling my ministry? Am I doing my job?"

God Will Save Anybody

For God so loved the world, that he gave his only begotten Son, that whosoever believeth in him should not perish, but have everlasting life.

John 3:16

God will save anybody. You need to keep reminding yourself, "God sent me— not somebody else—to tell them." God wants to save them, every one of them. It is our job to tell people about Jesus so they can be saved. If we don't do it, it won't get done.

Power of Jesus' Name

For God sent not his Son into the world to condemn the world; but that the world through him might be saved.

He that believeth on him is not condemned: but he that believeth not is condemned already, because he hath not believed in the name of the only begotten Son of God.

John 3:17,18

There is all power in Jesus' name. All you need to be an effective witness is the name of Jesus. When you open your mouth and mention to people that Name and the fact that Jesus loves them, the Spirit of God starts working on the inside of you because your spirit and that Name come together and start working together. God's presence is there when that Name is spoken. The Lord has shown us through the Scriptures what He will do for us if we will lift Him up and talk to others about Him. God's holy presence will be there to help you. Not one time will you ever be alone as long as you have the name of Jesus with you.

Wrought in God

And this is the condemnation, that light is come into the world, and men loved darkness rather than light, because their deeds were evil.

For every one that doeth evil hateth the light, neither cometh to the light, lest his deeds should be reproved.

Jesus Came to Save

> *But he that doeth truth cometh to the light, that his deeds may be made manifest, that they are wrought in God.*
>
> John 3:19-21

Jesus wants His deeds to be made manifest in you. When you become one spirit with God, you receive power to accomplish what you could not accomplish before of your own self. There are many different programs and techniques of witnessing. But if you will submit yourself to God, listen to His leading and allow His deeds to be made manifest in you, you will be surprised at the number of souls you will win.

Let me give you an example of how the Spirit of God can lead you in witnessing and provide the wisdom and power you need to handle whatever situation He places you in.

Not long ago I was in Florida at my little mission. One morning God woke me up about five o'clock. Now unless I'm going somewhere, I don't usually get up that early. But I woke up and couldn't go back to sleep, so I got up.

I showered, shaved, and got dressed. I went outside but nobody was up but me. It was still dark. I thought to myself, *What am I doing out here?* I didn't know exactly why but I had such a hunger in me to walk around the grounds and look at the buildings. So I started walking around the mission grounds. I knew within me that God wanted me there, but I didn't know why.

As I was walking around in front of the building, a car suddenly came up the highway. It circled the place, then pulled in the driveway and parked. In a minute or so, a police car pulled up and parked next to the curb. I saw a man get out of the car. I could tell that he was drunk, or pretty close to it, when he got closer to me. He said, "Mister, can I ask you a question?"

I said, "You can, if you want to."

He said, "Will you do me a favor?"

"What is it?"

"Would you please drive me home? I just left a bar a few minutes ago. I have been there all night drinking. The police told me when I came out that I had better not drive my car because I was too drunk. I waited until they left and started driving home anyway. I came up this way and I saw that they were following me so I came in here. If I get in my car and leave these grounds, they will arrest me."

The Holy Ghost started giving me words. I said, "You don't have to drink, you know. The Holy Ghost can dry you up. If you will give your life to Jesus Christ, the Holy Spirit will wash you white as snow and give you eternal life."

When I said that, he started crying. God hit him so strong that the police sitting in the car saw him fall. He fell down on his knees in front of me. He looked up to me with tears gushing out of his eyes and said, "Will you pray for me?"

I said, "Tell Jesus you're sorry for your sins."

He said, "I'm sorry for my sins."

So I started praying for him. Suddenly he jumped up and said, "I'm saved, I'm saved."

The Lord got me up at five o'clock in the morning to be a witness to a drunk. That's how important he was to God. God knew he was going to pull in there and He had me at the right spot at the right time so that fellow could see me and get saved.

To do that sort of thing, you have to be willing to get up at five o'clock in the morning. If you're not willing, God can't use you like that. You have to be willing to do what the Spirit of God says. You have to be willing to listen to what God is saying to you.

You Are God's Instrument

You meet all kinds of people when you're witnessing. That's the reason God wants to get your spirit in shape to witness to them—all kinds of them. That's why it is so important for you to realize that those who are born of the Spirit are spirit. When you go out there and witness for God, just understand that He is in you. Your spirit has been reborn by the Spirit of God. You are supposed to think like Him.

Now I don't mean that you are God, that you become the Holy Spirit; I am saying that you are spirit. The real you is a spirit being. You have a soul, and you live in a body, but you are a spirit. When your spirit gets born again by the Spirit of God, you take on the nature of God; you think and act like God thinks and acts. You then become God's instrument to reach others.

You Can Be A Soulwinner

But God can reach them through you only if you allow Him to do so. Let God witness through you. Jesus came to save. It is God's will to save. He will save anybody. Let Him use you. Be a witness. Be a soulwinner.

2
The Faithful Witness

God's power will do anything for you. But it doesn't just fall out of heaven on you. To have it, you must be willing to pay the price.

A person can live next door to a church all his life and never be saved unless somebody brings the message of salvation to him so he can receive it, believe it, and be reborn. In the same way, a person, even a born-again Christian, can be sick all his life and die unless he hears, receives, and believes the message of healing.

People will go on sitting in their homes, dying both physically and spiritually, until some Spirit-filled Christians pay the price to get them delivered. That's what witnessing is all about. The power of God is there to meet those needs; it is available. It *can* be yours. It *should* be yours. But it *won't* be yours until you pay the price it takes to have it.

Desperate needs cannot be met by "ordinary Christians." They just don't have the power it takes. Not because that power is not available to them, but because "ordinary Christians" won't put out the effort it takes to develop that power. Such Christians don't know what to do in really desperate situations like demon possession or fatal disease or drug addiction. They aren't prepared or equipped to handle things that extreme. But the Holy Ghost can get the job done. I've seen the Spirit of God do truly amazing things in people's lives. He will do it for you too, if you will pay the price to have the power.

There is only one way to deliver a person who is possessed of a demon: Go to him, lay hands on him in the name of Jesus Christ, and claim his deliverance. You must go there in the power and authority of the Holy Spirit of God. You must go with Jesus on your lips and victory in your mouth. You speak victory and it comes to pass. You tell the devil, "No, you don't! You can't have this man's mind! I won't let you have it! I know you'd like to keep it, but you're not going to, because I'm not going to let you!"

You have to speak to the devil to set people free from him. You have to tell him what he can and cannot do. Sweet, humble prayers by "ordinary Christians" won't get the job done. Deliverance comes by overpowering the devil, and that takes action as well as prayer.

The Destroyer

It is Satan's business to drive people crazy. It is his business to destroy. Jesus said that the devil comes for three reasons: to steal, to kill, and to destroy. (John 10:10.) He will steal anything from you. He'll destroy your mind, your body, your children, your business, your home, everything you have—if you let him. Satan destroys because that's his nature. All he has to do is to get you over into the sin business and he'll destroy you.

You see, sin is the devil's business. When you sin, you get into his territory. Sin separates a person from God, and sin will destroy you. If you get too far into sin, it will destroy your mind. So you have to watch yourself. When you see that something is going to damage you, back away from it.

Remember, when you were saved, it was your spirit, not your body, that got born again. Your physical body, your flesh, didn't get reborn. You are only born in the flesh one time. If you don't keep that physical body under subjection, it will drive you crazy. Yielding yourself to the wrong desires of your body, getting out of the will of God, will affect your mind. What you do to your body, and in your body, affects your mind and spirit. If you keep pushing your body, desiring carnal, fleshly things for it, sooner or later your mind will become affected. That is a spiritual law.

For example, there is alcohol. If a person fools around with alcohol, it will affect his mind and he will eventually become an alcoholic.

The same is true of drugs. It doesn't take long for a person to go from smoking marijuana to dropping pills. From there it's only one step to the needle and addiction.

If a person fools around with the devil for very long, he will end up becoming a slave to him. When a person becomes addicted to alcohol, drugs, homosexuality, abnormal sex acts, or any such thing, he has become a slave to Satan. He can no longer free himself; he must have God's help. It will take somebody who is strong in the knowledge and power of the Lord to set him free from that bondage. Otherwise the devil will kill him. That's where you and I come in. It's our job to help set people free. To do that, we must have the power of God. And that power comes only by being willing to pay the price. Being just an "ordinary Christian" will never be enough to set anyone free from bondage to Satan.

Spiritual Warfare

Whether you realize it or not, we are engaged in warfare—spiritual combat. There is a battle going on. If you are to gain the victory over the enemy and his demons, you must know how Satan operates.

About ten years ago I was speaking in a meeting in Jackson, Mississippi. As I was preaching, several people were sitting on the platform with me. I had been speaking for about seventeen minutes when suddenly the Spirit of the Lord fell on that place. When it did, a woman from the congregation began to speak in tongues—loud and long and clear. Kenneth Copeland, one of those on the platform, stood up and interpreted the message which was directed to me. Through Kenneth, God talked to me for about twenty minutes. God's power fell on the audience and they just rejoiced with me for the message which God brought forth.

The Faithful Witness

In essence, this is what He told me that night: "I'm going to bring your daughter back into the Kingdom of God. (She was away from the Lord at that time.) And I'm going to take authority over your finances. I'm going to bless you financially more than you've ever been blessed. Because you have yielded yourself totally to Me, because you stand on My Word and won't compromise, I'm going to take you into the devil's kingdom. I'm going to show you how Satan operates in the spirit realm. I'm going to show you this in three different manifestations."

That was about ten years ago. During the next three years, the Lord took me into those three manifestations. He took me out of my body, took me up into the air, and let me float through the air with demons. As a result of that experience, I know exactly how demons operate.

Demons are sort of like chicken hawks. They float through the air, seeking someone to devour. Demons work hard at trying to get you to yield yourself to temptation, to give in to some kind of sin, something that God doesn't want you to commit. If they can get you started into that particular sin, they will eventually take you over, because all they are doing is tempting you to yield yourself to them.

When you yield yourself to sin, whatever it may be, you're not just yielding to temptation—you're yielding yourself to a devil! It may be a lying devil, or a sex devil, or a drug devil, or an alcohol devil. It isn't sin you are yielding yourself to; it is Satan! Once that devil talks you into yielding yourself to him in that particular area, he will continue to ensnare you in that sin. If you keep going on into it, sooner or later you will become what that devil is.

That's why sin is so harmful to us as Christians. When we submit our bodies to sin, we are submitting our spirits to the devil and he gains power over us. He leads us into slavery to him. When we realize that we have done wrong, we must immediately stop ourselves.

Now you know when you have done wrong, don't you? Even an unsaved person knows when he has done wrong. God has put enough of His power into people just by creating them that they realize when they have sinned. No man, saved or unsaved, can make love to another man's wife and not know he has done wrong. He may not want to admit it, even to himself, but he knows.

No matter what they may try to tell themselves, people can't even get drunk without knowing they've done wrong. Their head will tell them that much, especially the next morning. They will wake up knowing how stupid they were for doing that.

When you yield yourself to whatever the devil has to offer you, you become over and over again what that spirit is. If you yield yourself to the bottle and get drunk a few times, you'll just keep on doing it until you either get saved or wind up being an alcoholic. That's when you become a slave to the devil. Thousands of Americans die every year because they are slaves of the devil.

Remember, you are engaged in spiritual warfare—a life or death battle. Don't fool around with the enemy; he will destroy you. Stay away from him. Resist him. Don't let him entice you into his trap. Stay away from him! Avoid even the appearance of evil. (1 Thess. 5:22.)

According to Your Knowledge

The problem with many churches today is they don't realize they are engaged in spiritual warfare. They just play around with the Lord and with their Bibles as though they were in some sort of game. Some people who call themselves Christians don't know the first thing about God. They talk about Him and tell people something about Him from the Scriptures, but they have no idea what God will do for them.

What will God do? He'll do anything for people. What will He do for the man who is paralyzed or demon possessed? He will do for that man according to your knowledge, if you minister to him. You'll only help people according to your knowledge of God.

It is never a question of what God will do for somebody. I'm telling you boldly: God will do anything for anybody. God's power is waiting to change the most twisted, ugly cripple in the world into a normal, healthy, beautiful person. But you have to know that, if you are to minister it. If you don't have that kind of knowledge, God can't work His miracles through you. God can only work through a person according to that person's knowledge of Him and his faith in Him. If you are to help people, you have to know what God will do for them—not what He **can** do, but what He **will** do. He will do anything for them.

But you also have to know **how** He will do it. It's not enough just to say, "Well, God can do anything, and I believe He will do it." You have to know how to do it! There are not two, or three, or four ways to get God to work a miracle. There is only one way — God's way. You have to find the scripture that covers that need, then pray and claim the victory in that situation until you see it come to pass.

Don't try to figure it out. The Holy Ghost is the only One Who has the intelligence to do that. But if you will do it, it will work, because God's Word works. God acts in response to faith in His Word, His promise. His Word will not come back to Him void. (Is. 55:11.) God will work with those who go out and work for Him.

If you aren't willing to pay the price, you won't get anything from God. But if you do pay the price, God will do anything for you.

The main problem with the Church today is that they get tired and lazy real easy. You can't help desperate cases by getting tired and lazy. You have to pay the price, or the power is not going to come. But if you'll pay the price, I guarantee that the power will come. God will do whatever you've asked Him to do, whatever you've claimed by faith in Jesus' name. God will perform any kind of miracle for you, if you'll pay the price to get it. But you must pay that price. There's no such thing as a cheap miracle.

Jesus Never Changes

To have the miracle power of God at work in you, the first thing you have to do is recognize that Jesus never changes. If you are to witness in power, you need to learn that. Jesus never changes.

Hebrews 13:8 says, *Jesus Christ* (is) *the same yesterday, and to day, and for ever.* Acts 10:34 tells us that *God is no respecter of persons.* What He has done for any of His children, He will do for you, if you will believe it.

If Jesus healed one person in the Bible, He will heal you, or anybody else who will believe Him. If He performed a miracle in the Scriptures, whatever that miracle may be, He will perform that same miracle for you—not somebody else, **you**—if you'll believe it.

There are those who will try to tell you that the age of miracles is past, that God worked miracles in the Bible for the "saints of old," but that He no longer operates that way today. Don't believe it! In Malachi 3:6 God declares, *I am the Lord, I change not.* God has not changed. Whatever He did for people then, He will do for people today.

> *And when his disciples were come to the other side, they had forgotten to take bread.*
>
> *Then Jesus said unto them, Take heed and beware of the leaven of the Pharisees and of the Sadducees.*
>
> *Matthew 16:5,6*

What Jesus was telling His disciples here is the same thing He is telling us today: "Don't listen to the doctrines of men." Don't listen to those who would try to tell you that God has changed, that He has quit doing miracles and has started working through doctors or lawyers or natural processes. God has not changed. Jesus Christ is the same—yesterday, today, and forever.

Don't Worry

And they reasoned among themselves, saying, It is because we have taken no bread.
Matthew 16:7

Now why should those disciples have been concerned and worried because they forgot to take bread? They had already forgotten who makes bread.

My friend, never think that you can't afford to take the time to go out and witness and minister for Jesus because you have "to make a living." Never worry about what you're going to eat, where you're going to live, what you're going to wear, how you're going to pay the bills. Don't worry about things like that. Let that be the least of your worries. As long as you belong to God and are bringing souls into the kingdom of heaven, you will be provided for. God has promised you that. (Matt. 6:25-34.) As long as you obey God, go out into the hedges and byways, and compel sinners to come to Him, God will speak to people and have them bring bread to your door. If He has to, He'll have the birds come to your house and feed you just like He did for the prophet of old. (1 Kings 17:2-6.)

God says not to worry about what you're going to eat or where you're going to sleep. Don't worry about anything like that. Christians aren't supposed to be concerned about how much money they made last year or how much they are going to make this year. They're supposed to be concerned about how many souls they won for God last year and how many they are going to win this year.

Did you talk to anybody about Jesus last month? If you didn't, start. If you will do that for God, He will do anything for you. But He won't do anything for you as long as you do your own thing the way you want to do it. You cause God to lift His blessings from you because of your laziness.

God doesn't bless stingy people and lazy people. If you don't believe that, just become stingy and lazy, then see what happens. You'll have the curse of the world on you. All kinds of things will come on you because you aren't fruitful for God. But as long as you bring fruit into the kingdom of heaven, God will do anything for you. Your mind and spirit can stay free because you're giving out the Word of God to people.

The greatest thing that can happen for you and for others is for you to open your mouth and share the Gospel of Jesus Christ. When you do that, both of you get blessed—you and the person you share the Lord with. If you want God's blessing flowing in, start letting His Gospel flow out!

Have You Forgotten?

Which when Jesus perceived, he said unto them, O ye of little faith, why reason ye among

> *yourselves, because ye have brought no bread?*
>
> *Do ye not yet understand, neither remember the five loaves of the five thousand, and how many baskets ye took up?*
> Matthew 16:8,9

Have you lost your memory? Do you know what the Lord says to a church when cripples come in and go out still crippled? Do you know what Jesus says to His people when they refuse to lay hands on the sick and pray for them? Jesus is crying out to His Church: "O Church, have you forgotten Who I am? Why don't you read Matthew, Mark, Luke, and John to see how I heal crippled people? Why don't you lay hands on them, O ye of little faith?"

The laying on of hands is a commandment of Jesus with which the Church of Jesus Christ has to come to grips. If a church doesn't lay hands on people and pray for them in Jesus' name, then that church has forgotten the Lord they serve and how He ministered.

Too many churches think the way I used to think when I was sold out to a denomination: "Well, that's not the way we do things at our church, and we have the biggest and best church in town. Our pastor has a doctorate, and our assistant pastor graduated from the seminary. You ought to come up to our church. We have the most beautiful sanctuary, the most gorgeous stained-glass windows, the tallest steeple, the best organized program, the most talented choir director, the softest pew cushions, and the best sound system of any church in this city. You ought to come to our Wednesday night church supper. Our dining room staff whips up the best meals you've ever tasted! Yes, sir, we have a number-one church!"

People ask me, "Well, did you like to go to church there?"

I tell them, "Oh, yes, I loved to go there. They didn't require anything of me." Why not? Because they didn't require anything of themselves. If you don't do anything yourself, you're not likely to require anything of anybody else.

If the pastor of your church doesn't cast out devils, then he isn't going to require you to do that either. If your church staff doesn't lay hands on the sick and pray for their healing, they won't expect you to. You won't have to do anything your church leaders don't do. But you also won't have any more power than they have. All you'll ever be able to do for the sick and demon possessed is just what your leaders do: Bow very reverently and humbly pray, "O Lord, heal this person, if it be Thy will."

Praying like that is a waste of time and breath. If you don't know what God's will is before you pray, there's no use praying.

Don't pray, "If it be Thy will." **The Bible is God's will!** Get the will down and read it yourself! Find out what God's will is, then pray it! Never pray **about** the Bible—it's already true. Just read it and believe it. Don't read something from the Bible, then pray, "O God, if it's Thy will, give me this blessing in Matthew or this blessing in Mark. O God, if it's Thy will, let me have this blessing that I read about in

Romans." No! You will never get anything praying like that!

Who do you think the Bible was written for? The devil? No! It's yours—all of it! You just need to read God's will, then pray according to that will, according to what He has already provided for you. Don't forget who you are and Who your Father is.

> Bless the Lord, O my soul, and forget not all his benefits:
>
> Who forgiveth all thine iniquities; who healeth all thy diseases;
>
> Who redeemeth thy life from destruction; who crowneth thee with lovingkindness and tender mercies;
>
> Who satisfieth thy mouth with good things; so that thy youth is renewed like the eagle's.
>
> Psalm 103:2-5

Beware of the Doctrines of Men

> Do ye not yet understand, neither remember the five loaves of the five thousand, and how many baskets ye took up? Neither the seven loaves of the four thousand, and how many baskets ye took up?
>
> How is it that ye do not understand that I spake it not to you concerning bread, that ye should beware of the leaven of the Pharisees and of the Sadducees?

> *Then understood they how that he bade them not beware of the leaven of bread, but of the doctrine of the Pharisees and of the Sadducees.*
>
> Matthew 16:9-12

We must beware of the doctrines of men—all men. Jesus is the Head of the Church. We must listen to Him. If you listen to Him, you won't try to change Him.

"Change Jesus? How do we try to change Him?"

Any time we take His Word and interpret it to suit our own ideas or church creeds and doctrines, we are trying to change the Lord. We can't make His Word conform to our ideas, beliefs, opinions, or experiences. We make all these things conform to His Word. Jesus doesn't change; we change. We *grow up into him in all things, which is the head, even Christ* (Eph. 4:15).

Remember Who He Is

> *When Jesus came into the coasts of Caesarea Philippi, he asked his disciples, saying, Whom do men say that I the Son of man am?*
>
> *And they said, Some say that thou art John the Baptist: some, Elias; and others, Jeremias, or one of the prophets.*
>
> *He saith unto them, But whom say ye that I am?*

> And Simon Peter answered and said, Thou art the Christ, the Son of the Living God.
>
> Matthew 16:13-16

If you want to be a good witness for Jesus, never forget Who He is. I don't care how far into sin a person has gone or what kind of miracle he may need, He can reach that person and meet his need. Never forget Who Jesus is.

The Church Victorious

> And Jesus answered and said unto him, Blessed art thou, Simon Barjona: for flesh and blood hath not revealed it unto thee, but my Father which is in heaven.
>
> And I say also unto thee, That thou art Peter, and upon this rock I will build my church; and the gates of hell shall not prevail against it.
>
> And I will give unto thee the keys of the kingdom of heaven: and whatsoever thou shalt bind on earth shall be bound in heaven: and whatsoever thou shalt loose on earth shall be loosed in heaven.
>
> Matthew 16:17-19

There is no defeat for the Church that Jesus built. Jesus said the gates of hell will not prevail against it. If the Church of Jesus Christ will hold forth the Word of God, it won't fail or be defeated; it will triumph in every case. There is no defeat in Jesus Christ because His Word will never fail. If the Church will preach that Word, it will reap the benefits of it.

The Faithful Witness

God will move in response to those who are faithful enough to stand in the gap and witness for Him. Let me give you an example.

I used to work with a man who had been in the penitentiary about six times. He had been on dope for years. When he came home on probation after his sixth term, he hardly knew his own children. One day his sixteen-year-old daughter found him pacing the floor like a hungry tiger. She said, "Daddy, why don't you relax and have a good time?"

"Honey, I can't. I don't want to go back to prison, but I know I'm going to. I can feel it coming on."

"Daddy, you don't have to go back. I hardly know you. You only come home between prison terms. I don't want you to go back. Why don't you go to church with Mama?"

"Church? Honey, that's for your mother. People like me don't go to church."

"Daddy, I've only been with you about three years of my life, and I'm sixteen years old. I don't know you very well, but you're a nice daddy when you're home. Why don't you stay out of that gang? Stay here with us."

"I'd like to, but I can't. It gets to me. When that old craving for whiskey and dope and money comes back on me, I can't stand it."

"Daddy, since you've been home, have you noticed those big corns and calluses on Mama's knees? She got those by being on her knees in the Assembly of God Church, praying for you. Every Sunday when the pastor dismissed the service, she would go to the altar and pray until two or three o'clock in the afternoon. Daddy, she prayed for you every Sunday. She had to work at the laundry all through the week for fourteen dollars. Every Sunday she would put her tithe of $1.40 in an envelope. She could have gone to the courthouse, given them one dollar, and been legally divorced from you. Then she would have been free to marry someone who would provide for her. Her Christian brothers and sisters tried to get her to do it, but she wouldn't. She said the Lord told her to stand in the gap for you, that He would bring you into the Kingdom and use you.''

Then she pleaded with him, ''Please, Daddy, go to church with Mama, and you'll change.'' Now that is the witness of a person who hasn't forgotten Who Jesus is and what He can do.

''I'd like to change, honey, but I just can't.''

''But you'll change, Daddy, if you go to church. Jesus will change you. He changes people. You can be like Mama.''

The daughter kept talking until that man came under conviction and agreed to go to church with his family. Once he had promised, he couldn't back out. The gang he was part of had taught him that there were two things he couldn't do: He couldn't make out with the gangsters' girlfriends, and he couldn't tell a lie in the gang. Anyone who dared lie to the

The Faithful Witness

other gang members ended up dead—no questions asked, no trial, no second chances. He just disappeared and was never heard of again.

When this man finally broke down and promised his daughter that he would go to church, he had to keep his word, even if he really didn't want to go. He went to church and the preacher seemed to preach right to him. At the invitation, he got up out of his seat and walked to the front of the church. He knelt down and said, "God, if You don't do something for me, I'll be eternally lost. If You don't help me, I'll go back to prison and be doomed forever. You have to do something for me tonight, God."

All of a sudden, the presence of God swept through him. That old burden of sin rolled away and he was made a brand new creature. The Spirit of God set him on fire for the Lord!

He became what God told his wife he would be, and it happened because his wife and daughter were faithful witnesses. His wife was faithful to stand in the gap Sunday after Sunday praying for him to be saved and transformed. His daughter was faithful to witness to him—to tell him Who Jesus is and what He would do for him.

One of the easiest things for a human being to do is to forget Who Jesus is and what He will do. Well, I have good news for you. Jesus will do anything you believe Him to do—anything!

Let Him do something for you and for those around you in need. Be a faithful witness and unleash God's power in your life and theirs.

3
Ordained to Witness

To be an effective witness for Jesus Christ, it is important to flow with the Spirit of God. A one-time experience with the Lord isn't enough. You have to stay in the flow of God's Spirit.

I can give you a good example of what I am talking about. I knew a young man named Mike who was a homosexual until he was delivered when I laid hands on him. After I had cast the demon of homosexuality out of him and God had filled him with His Spirit, the Lord revealed to me what would happen if Mike didn't remain strong in the Lord.

The Lord said to me, "If this young man ever leaves your ministry before he gets strong enough to take care of himself, his old desires will come back on him and he'll go back to his old habits and life."

I told Mike what the Lord had said: "Mike, if you ever leave me before you get strong enough to withstand temptation, you'll backslide. If you ever get off the road of campus ministry, Satan will tempt you back into the old life. God said that He wants you to keep moving from city to city until He has gotten you strong."

You have to understand what a homosexual is. It is like being an alcoholic. You have to keep your mind and spirit occupied, else the temptation will overcome you. You have to keep moving fast so you don't get too involved with people. If you stay in one place too long, you can become involved with the wrong kind of people again. That is how the devil operates. You can't hang around the devil and stay pure. You have to make up your mind to get away from the devil's territory permanently.

One Christmas Mike left the road and it happened. He got into trouble; but, thank God, he came back to the Lord.

Necessity of Commitment

The easiest thing in the world for people to do is to go to hell. If you want to go to heaven, you have to work at it. It is very easy to wind up in hell. Just get tired of the Gospel, get tired of going to church, get tired of Jesus, get tired of praying to God, start doing your own thing, and you're on the road to hell right then. You can't turn against Jesus and go to heaven. You have to keep yourself in the presence of God. How do you do that? By prayer. You pray yourself into victory, into the presence of God.

If you feel yourself getting weak, having "up days" and "down days," you need to spend more time in prayer. You have become lazy and lax about your prayer life and your commitment. Unless that is corrected, you are headed for trouble.

You have to make yourself pray. Once you get a strong foundation of God's Word in you, make up your mind that you are going to win souls for God and determine to work for God all the days of your life; then you are on pretty fair ground. But you have to make up your mind to stay away from the wrong kind of people. You have to determine that, regardless of what others may do, you are going to serve God.

To be an effective witness, operating in the wisdom and power of God, you have to be totally committed. A half-hearted resolve will never be enough to meet the challenges and overcome the obstacles you will face.

You will have to spend time in prayer and meditation in God's Word. You should also associate with other strong Christians who are successful soul-winners, people who can guide you and strengthen you as you learn to witness with wisdom and power.

Remember, God does not bless ignorance, nor does He bless laziness. God blesses faith and obedience.

When things get a little tough, you may be tempted to say, "Well, I don't know if God has called me to this ministry or not." That statement shows ignorance. Who do you think He wrote the Bible for? He didn't write it just for me or for someone else. He wrote it for you! When He says to go into all the world and preach the Gospel to every creature, He meant just what He said—and He meant it for you. It is up to you to do what God has specifically commanded you to do—whether other people do it or not, whether they approve or not, whether they even understand or not.

Your job is to read the Bible, study it, learn it, and spend time in God's presence communing with Him. Then you are to go out and do what He told you to do. You are ordained to witness, but to do that takes commitment. It takes devotion. It requires faith and obedience. **But it also pays.**

Increasing Your Effectiveness

Twenty years ago when I gave my life to the Lord, I made up my mind that I was going to obey God whatever the cost. As I did, He led me into greater responsibility and blessings.

As you accept God's commands and carry them out, He will increase your ability and effectiveness. As God can trust you more, He will exalt and promote you. He will put you in charge of more and more, because you will have proven yourself faithful in the little things. I know this is true because I ministered for about eight years in the ministry of helps and certain other things before God put His power in my hands to pray for the sick and see them healed. Now that power comes every time I teach or pray or talk about it. I can just start talking about healing scriptures and about the laying on of hands, and the power starts coming into my hands. My fingers begin to tingle as the Spirit of God begins to flow into my hands. Then I can lay hands on the sick and God will perform special miracles for them.

If you want to receive God's power, then believe God's Word and obey His instructions. Be a faithful witness and God will honor that commitment by increasing your power and ability.

They Shall Lay Hands on the Sick

And God wrought special miracles by the hands of Paul.

Acts 19:11

It was God Who worked the miracles, not Paul. God works miracles by the hands of His servants.

"Well, I don't think that is necessary," some might say. "I think I'll just pray; that'll be enough."

The Bible doesn't say that special miracles were wrought by the *prayers* of Paul. It says, *God wrought special miracles by the hands of Paul.* Laying hands on people is a doctrine of the Church, just like water baptism.

If you are going to minister as a Full Gospel Christian—if you are going to listen to God and obey God—you have no choice but to lay hands on people.

Any church that does not lay hands on the sick and minister to those in need is out of God's will. Churches are not supposed to be run by men; they are supposed to take orders from God. If the Church will do what God says to do, the Holy Presence will sweep in and bless people mightily. Men are not qualified to run the Church. Jesus Christ is the Head of the Church. We must be obedient to Him if we are to be blessed ourselves and are to be a blessing to others.

We Should Obey God, Not Men

So that from his body were brought unto the sick handkerchiefs or aprons, and the diseases departed from them, and the evil spirits went out of them.

Acts 19:12

This is the scriptural basis for anointing cloths and the reason we place prayer cloths on sick bodies to make devils and disease disappear. God's Holy Spirit is so powerful when you do what God tells you to do. It's a matter of obedience to God. Many times men don't understand. They belittle the practice of using prayer cloths and laugh at those who believe in it. Don't ever be influenced by unbelief. We are not to obey men; we are to obey God. When we place anointing cloths on the sick and pray for them, we are following the example set for us by the Apostle Paul. We are being obedient to God's revealed Word, and our faith and obedience will be honored by God.

Stay in the Flow

If you want to be a truly effective witness and minister, you need to be part of a church where the Spirit of God reigns and is allowed to flow freely. Never get yourself involved in a cold church. It is too easy to backslide there. You have to stay in a place where the Spirit of God flows sweetly and gently. That Spirit is your power, more precious to you than gold. That's why it is so important to stick close to the Spirit of God, to stick close to a place where the Spirit of God is.

Be Faithful

Elisha asked the prophet Elijah for a double portion of the Spirit, of the anointing that rested upon him. (2 Kings 2:9.) Elijah said to him, *Thou hast asked a hard thing: nevertheless, if thou see me when I am taken from thee, it shall be so unto thee . . .* (2 Kings 2:10). In other words, Elijah was saying, "If you'll stick close to me, if you're right there at the moment I go up into heaven, you'll receive it." If we want God's power and anointing, we must stick close to Him.

If you study these scriptures, you will see that Elisha made up his mind to stick to Elijah everywhere he went. When God would tell Elijah to go somewhere, Elijah would tell Elisha, "Now you don't have to go." But Elisha would always answer, *As the Lord liveth, and as thy soul liveth, I will not leave thee* (vv. 2,4,6). He stuck close to Elijah. Wherever God sent Elijah, Elisha would be right there with him.

Now what we are talking about here is faithfulness—being faithful **for a long period of time.** Elijah was saying to Elisha, "Because you have been faithful all these years and have trod the path to these cities with me, you are going to take my place when I'm gone. When I leave, if you are standing close to me and are faithful to the end, my anointing will be imparted to you. But you have to be close to receive it."

Friend, you must stay close to God in order to move in the power of God. You can't be lazy and still operate in God's anointing.

"Well, I know God. I'm a Christian. So God's blessings will be mine and the Lord will have His way."

No, the only time the Lord will have His way with you is when you believe the Bible, pray, and refuse to be lazy. God doesn't have His way with lazy people. They never win any souls. If people won't give their money to God's work, God doesn't have a chance to open the windows of heaven and pour out a blessing upon them. We only receive from God in proportion to what we have put in His work. . . . *For with the same measure that ye mete withal it shall be measured to you again* (Luke 6:38).

Ten years ago God told me in a prophecy, "Son, if you keep walking with Me like you are walking now, I'm going to bless you in every way. I'm going to bless you in the same measure as your faithfulness and obedience. When I get through blessing you, people will know you have been in My Presence because otherwise you couldn't have received such blessings."

Those blessings are already flowing. They flow to me like a river. I don't try to work at receiving God's blessing or try to make it happen. I just keep passing out tracts, keep witnessing, keep giving my life to God, keep praying, keep casting out devils, and keep giving out the Gospel. As I do, God's blessing keeps flowing to me. Why does God's blessing fall so freely upon me? Because the Lord said it would, in proportion to my faithfulness.

And He will cause the same to happen for anyone who will pay the price of faithful service. *Seek ye first the kingdom of God, and his righteousness; and all these things shall be added unto you* (Matt. 6:33).

But what if I were to get lazy and say to myself, "I'm not going to pass out any more tracts. My ministry has progressed beyond that. I'm too important a person to fool with that kind of thing. I have six hundred invitations in my office right now. Big churches want me to speak to them. I can pull in some big offerings that way. Just think how much good I could do with all that money. I can't afford to waste my valuable time by handing out tracts on the street corner or visiting sick folks in the hospital or trying to help some drunk on skid row. I'm too big and important to mess around with that sort of thing." If that happened, I wouldn't be big and important very long!

But, you see, I'm not going to make that mistake. I know better. I would rather go where the Spirit of God wants me to go and get a small offering, than go to a place just for the money I could get.

I understand that when you have a ministry it is nice to receive large offerings to meet all those expenses. I like it myself. But if that is **all** you are going for, if that offering takes the place of the leadership and anointing of God, look out! That's not where it's at. You can't start thinking of yourself as a big shot and expect to work for God. When God calls you to do something, just go ahead and do it. Don't become puffed up with your own self-importance.

One year the Lord said to me, "Son, I want you to help some poor people at Christmas." To be perfectly honest, I didn't want to spend Christmas doing just that. But I did it. I spent Christmas Day carrying food to poor families from our little mission in Florida. That was the greatest Christmas I have ever spent in my life!

When God talks, listen to Him, and then be faithful to do what He has asked you to do. He knows exactly how to give you blessings. As you go out to witness and minister, let the Spirit of God flow through you. You will have success, and it will bless you as much as, or more than, it blesses those you minister to.

Ministering in Jesus' Name

And now, Lord, behold their threatenings: and grant unto thy servants, that with all boldness they may speak thy word, by stretching forth thine hand to heal; and that signs and wonders may be done by the name of thy holy child Jesus.

And when they had prayed, the place was shaken where they were assembled together; and they were all filled with the Holy Ghost, and they spake the word of God with boldness.
                                    Acts 4:29-31

We recognize this as the prayer the disciples prayed after Peter and John had been released from prison where they had been held for healing the lame man at the gate of the temple.

Do you remember the defense Peter and John gave when questioned by the high priest? When he asked them, *By what power, or by what name, have ye done this?* (Acts 4:7), what did they answer?

> *Then Peter, filled with the Holy Ghost, said unto them, Ye rulers of the people, and elders of Israel, if we this day be examined of the good deed done to the impotent man, by what means he is made whole;*
>
> *Be it known unto you all, and to all the people of Israel, that by the name of Jesus Christ of Nazareth, whom ye crucified, whom God raised from the dead, even by him doth this man stand here before you whole.*
>
> Acts 4:8-10

Everything that you are called to do, you are to do in the name of Jesus Christ. We must live and move and have our being in Him. We must work and minister in His name. It is the name of Jesus which empowers us to meet the needs of those to whom we go to witness.

Some will say, "But that power is just for certain people. That doesn't mean me, Brother Norvel." Let's look in Mark 16 and see if it does:

> *. . . Go ye into all the world, and preach the Gospel to every creature. He that believeth and is baptized shall be saved; but he that believeth not shall be damned.*
>
> *And these signs shall follow them that believe; In my name shall they cast out devils; they shall speak with new tongues; they shall take up serpents; and if they drink any deadly*

> *thing, it shall not hurt them; they shall lay hands on the sick, and they shall recover.*
> *Mark 16:15-18*

Who did Jesus say would accomplish these things? "Them that believe." Do you believe? If you do, then this includes you. You are called to cast out devils and to lay hands on the sick.

You might say, "But we don't do that in our church."

Well, they didn't do that in the church I went to either. I had to learn it in another church. You can't learn to do that where it is not preached or believed or practiced. You have to leave that church and go where they do preach and practice it.

God sent me to a Pentecostal church. I sat there and I watched. Then it wasn't long until the pastor looked down at me and said, "Come up here, Brother Norvel, and let's pray for these people." I had never prayed like that before in my life, but I tried it. I watched the Pentecostals and did what they did.

One night as I was at the altar praying, my fingers began to tingle. I walked over to the pastor and said, "Pastor, what's wrong with my hands? It feels like the bones are going to jump out of my fingers."

The pastor said, "Brother Norvel, Sister So-and-So is here at the altar. She has been real sick lately. Come over here right now and lay your hands on her."

I went over to her, laid my hands on her in the name of Jesus, and she just fell over on the floor! Now that can scare a Baptist the first time it happens! It scared me! But God can put His healing power in people's hands if He wants to.

You stay faithful to God and He will put His power into your hands.

Ordained to Witness

Many times when I walk into a room and pray for a person, he will just break down and start to weep. To develop that kind of power, you have to stick close to a person or a ministry who will help you develop and grow.

I would like to be the person to help you through these pages to enter into the ministry of witnessing in power to the needs of those around you. Any good thing that God has put in my spirit over the years, I'm going to ask Him to begin to let flow into you right now. I'm going to ask God to strengthen any part of your life that's weak and fill it with His power. As I pray for you, receive God's power and calling upon your life. Lay your hands on this book and in sincerity open your heart to God to be filled with His anointing.

Father, in the name of the Lord Jesus Christ, I come to You now confessing my sins and asking You to forgive me and to cleanse me without and within.

I ask You, Lord, to take away from me anything that's not good. Let everything in me be pure and clean and holy. Let Your holy presence flow from these pages into the person holding this book whose heart is open to receive Your power and anointing.

I pray, Lord, that any good thing You have put in me to minister with will flow from me into the one reading these words. May he or she be filled with Your Holy Spirit and empowered to do Your will.

Keep this person strong and free so that he or she can lift those who are weak out of darkness and set them in Your marvelous light so they too may be set free.

In Jesus' name, I impart Your power, grace, and peace to the one who reads this. I thank You that it is done now in the precious and powerful name of Your Holy Child, Jesus Christ. Amen.

Now receive that anointing from God and begin to minister in it. Go forth to share with others the Lord Jesus Christ. You are ordained of God to witness and commissioned to go and teach all nations. . . . *and, lo,* (He is) *with you alway, even unto the end of the world* (Matt. 28:20).

4
Witnessing With Authority

Then he (Jesus) called his twelve disciples together, and gave them power and authority over all devils, and to cure diseases.

And he sent them to preach the kingdom of God, and to heal the sick.
Luke 9:1,2

We see here the scriptural basis for laying hands on people and imparting to them anything that God has given us to minister with, including authority over devils and power to cure diseases. We do that because that is what the Lord did right here. *He called his twelve disciples together, and gave them power and authority over all devils, and to cure diseases.*

In Matthew 28:18,19 we read the words Jesus said to His disciples just before He ascended into heaven:

All power is given unto me in heaven and in earth. Go ye therefore . . . .

Jesus is the One Who had authority and power over all devils, and He has given that power to us,

His disciples. When we go to witness and minister, we go in the power and authority of the Lord Jesus Christ. Not only are we *ordained* to witness, we are also *empowered* to witness.

Witnessing With Power

> *But he (Jesus) passing through the midst of them went his way, and came down to Capernaum, a city of Galilee, and taught them on the sabbath days.*
>
> *And they were astonished at his doctrine: for his word was with power.*
> Luke 4:30-32

When you witness, let your words be full of love and full of power. Know that you know that you know what you are talking about. Don't let people or the devil talk you out of it. Your spirit, your mind, your eyes, and your mouth can be full of success and power and authority—if you will pray before you go out. To do God's work, make sure you are full of God's Spirit.

Casting Out Devils

> *And in the synagogue there was a man, which had a spirit of an unclean devil, and cried out with a loud voice,*
>
> *Saying, Let us alone; what have we to do with thee, thou Jesus of Nazareth? art thou come to destroy us? I know thee who thou art; the Holy One of God.*

> *And Jesus rebuked him, saying, Hold thy peace, and come out of him. And when the devil had thrown him in the midst, he came out of him, and hurt him not.*
>
> Luke 4:33-35

Learn how to cast out devils. Jesus taught me how and He'll teach you, too, if you'll let Him.

Speak to the devil and order him to depart, in the name of Jesus. If a person is afraid, say, "Spirit of fear, in Jesus' name, come out." Break it loose; make it leave. You make it come out—not somebody else, **you.**

You might say, "Well, God will make it come out if He wants it out." No, He won't. Just as Jesus came to do the will of His Father, so He has sent us to do that will. God wants that evil spirit driven out, just as He did in Jesus' day, but He accomplished that will through Jesus. Now He accomplishes that will through us, through me and you.

You say, "Well, Jesus can cast it out." No, He has quit ministering in the flesh. We are now the Body of Christ. He doesn't cast out devils anymore; we do. Jesus is in heaven sitting at the right hand of God. He said very plainly in Mark 16:17: *And these signs shall follow them that believe; In my name shall they cast out devils* . . . . If you believe in Jesus, that refers to you. It isn't the Lord's business anymore to cast out devils; it's your business to cast them out.

"But my friends and relatives will think I'm strange, won't they?"

Yes, they will. But you have to reach the place in your life where you obey God regardless of what the world thinks. I don't care what you or anybody else believes. What other people think doesn't influence me one bit. If you are going to worry about what people think or believe, you will be harassed by devils for the rest of your life. You'll wind up doing nothing, especially in your own hometown.

Go and Possess the Land

Jesus told me one time, "Remember, son, people only believe what they have been taught. So teach My people the Bible."

My friend, God wants you to believe the Bible. Most people will say that they believe the Bible but they don't. They just think they do. They haven't even read it and have no earthly idea what it says.

If you aren't a Bible reader, you would be amazed at the truth of God's Word, at all the authority and power you possess as a child of God, at all the things the Holy Spirit wants to do for you and your family, at the enormous price Jesus paid for you to have the abundant life. God wants you to possess it, so go and possess the land! (Deut. 1:21.)

God is saying to His people: "If you can see it, take it for God." Just make sure that you are scriptural. Casting out devils—repossessing human minds, bodies and spirits—most certainly is scriptural. That's what Jesus came to do, and that's what He has sent us to do.

Ministering Everywhere

> *And they were all amazed, and spake among themselves, saying, What a word is this! for with authority and power he commandeth the unclean spirits, and they come out.*
>
> *And the fame of him went out into every place of the country round about.*
>
> Luke 4:36,37

Jesus has conferred that same authority and power upon us to continue His work on this earth now. He cast out devils in church. Why then is the Church not doing that today?

Now let's see what happened when Jesus left church. Where did He go and what did He do?

> *And he arose out of the synagogue, and entered into Simon's house. And Simon's wife's mother was taken with a great fever; and they besought him for her.*
>
> *And he stood over her, and rebuked the fever; and it left her: and immediately she arose and ministered unto them.*
>
> Luke 4:38,39

Obviously Jesus' ministry was not confined to the inside of the church. He went into people's homes, out into the streets and highways, and into public places. Peter tells us: . . . *God anointed Jesus of Nazareth with the Holy Ghost and with power: who went about* (everywhere) *doing good, and healing all that were oppressed of the devil; for God was with him* (Acts 10:38).

Has God anointed *you* with the Holy Ghost? For what purpose? So you too can go about everywhere doing good and healing all that are oppressed of the devil. How could Jesus accomplish all this? . . . *for God was with him.* Has God promised to be with you? Then there is no reason why you can't accomplish the same things Jesus did.

I Would Not Have You Ignorant

Notice that Jesus went into Simon's house, stood over Simon's mother-in-law, and rebuked the fever. (Luke 4:39.) Does that mean Jesus actually stood over somebody's bed and spoke to a fever like it was a person?

Well, that's how you get rid of it. I have done that lots of times with fever. Many times a person is out of his head with fever, so some member of the family will call me to come and minister to him. It has become a life-or-death situation. Those people wouldn't have to call me if they knew what to do themselves. But if you are ignorant yourself, you'd better call somebody who isn't ignorant, or you may wind up like my mother, dead before your time.

Our family attended a Southern Baptist church all our lives. At age thirty-seven, my mother developed cancer. I was ten, my sister was eleven, and my brother was fourteen. The church put my mother's name on a blackboard so the people could pray for her. We couldn't obey James 5:14,15 because we had no oil to anoint people with. We couldn't obey Mark 16 because we had no healing services and did not practice the laying on of hands as taught by Jesus.

Some people say it doesn't matter where you go to church as long as you go. That's just not so. Where you go to church determines what you are taught to believe; and what you are taught to believe determines whether you live or die, spiritually **and** physically. My mother's church affiliation was important, deadly important. So is yours. If you get cancer, it will cost you your life if you don't go someplace where they believe that there is all power and all authority in Jesus' name. Salvation, healing, health, prosperity, peace, power, success—all these things are available for those who believe and will exercise their authority to possess them.

The devil is here to steal, to kill, and to destroy. (John 10:10.) He is the one who causes you harm. You have to learn to take authority over him.

Using the Name of Jesus

Consider a small thing like fever. What kind of action did Jesus take against fever? He rebuked the fever in Simon's mother-in-law, and it left her.

What would you do for it? You should do the same thing. Anything that I can do, in Jesus' name, you can do. I'm not some kind of super-saint with a supernatural power available only to me. I'm not greater than you. Any power I have, you have. If you've been born again by the Spirit of God, you have the right to use the name of Jesus just as much as I do. Either you do it, or you don't.

The difference between me and most other folks in the Church, the reason I have power and authority that they don't have, is simple: I believe and act; they don't. I use the name of Jesus.

If you call my house and ask me to come minister to a member of your family who is out of his mind with fever, I will do it. I will stand beside that person's bed, just like Jesus did, and rebuke that fever in Jesus' name. I will stand there and rebuke it until it breaks and leaves. And you can do the same thing.

Your head will tell you, "But, Brother Norvel, I don't know how to do that."

Yes, you do. I just told you. Besides that, the Gospel of Luke tells you. You can read it for yourself. Why do you think God put those scriptures in the Bible? He put them there to teach you what to do. The Lord Jesus Christ wants you and all believers to do what He did.

Jesus is the Great Shepherd, and He knows exactly what He is talking about. He knows exactly what He is doing in every case. He knows exactly what to do to get anyone saved or healed or delivered. It's a shame that the Church doesn't know that, but Jesus does. All you have to do is to follow after Jesus, say what He said, and do what He did the way He did it.

You have the authority to use Jesus' name. His name and power and authority have been given to the Church. That means you! You do the things Jesus did and the God Who confirmed the ministry of Jesus will confirm your ministry because you are doing it in Jesus' name.

Witnessing With Authority

Do you have cancer or disease or infirmity in your body right now? If so, just use the name of Jesus and speak to it with power and authority: "You foul affliction, in Jesus' name, come out of my body. Cancer, disease, infirmity, I take authority over you. I curse you, in Jesus' name. Die! Get out of my body, in the name of Jesus Christ of Nazareth!"

Nothing can stay in your body if you order it to leave, in Jesus' name. But if you are going to fool around, getting people to pray for you, spending all your money on doctors and different kinds of cures, sitting around feeling sorry for yourself, it won't work.

You had better learn to be a witness with power and authority. You can go to people's houses and help them if you are a witness with power and authority. If you know what to do, you can give them instructions and help to set them free from Satan's bondage. But you have to be able to help yourself before you can help somebody else.

The Gospel works for anybody, and it will work for you—if you will believe it and act on it!

Receiving the Power

And he stood over her, and rebuked the fever; and it left her (Luke 4:39). Now is that hard to understand? Notice the result. The Bible says, . . . *and immediately she arose and ministered unto them.* Immediately. That is the opposite of waiting a while, isn't it? She got up immediately and started ministering. Speaking the Word and speaking the name of Jesus gets immediate results!

> *Now when the sun was setting, all they that had any sick with divers diseases brought them unto him; and he laid his hands on every one of them, and healed them.*
>
> *Luke 4:40*

Everybody in that town who had anybody sick in their household brought them to Jesus. He laid His hands on every one of them and healed them. He healed them all—every one of them.

You may ask, "How could Jesus have that much power in His hands?"

Because He prayed all night and lived a clean life. You and I are kind of lazy. We don't pray all night like Jesus did. You and I pray fifteen minutes—maybe—then wonder why we lack power. You can have all of God's power you can stand, but you have to pay the price to get it. Go before God. Seek God and pray. The power will come—and that power is what makes the difference.

The devil is a thief, and he'll rob you of everything you have if you let him. You have to take authority over him. Every time he tries to attack you or any member of your family, rebuke him. Say, "Satan, I take authority over you, in the name of Jesus. You foul devil, I'll not allow you to rob me. Take your demons and depart right now. I rebuke you. Get out, in the name of Jesus Christ!" *Resist the devil, and he will flee from you* (James 4:7).

When you go out to witness, do so in the power and authority of the name of Jesus Christ. That is your right and your responsibility.

5
Witnessing in Love

Then there arose a reasoning among them (the disciples), *which of them should be greatest.*

And Jesus, perceiving the thought of their heart, took a child, and set him by him, and said unto them, Whosoever shall receive this child in my name receiveth me: and whosoever shall receive me receiveth him that sent me: for he that is least among you all, the same shall be great.

Luke 9:46-48

There is a danger in witnessing and ministering, but the danger is not defeat. If you go in the power and authority of God, you will not be defeated. Satan can't stop you. If you are faithful and keep at it, you will succeed.

The danger is not defeat; it is pride and conceit—an overestimation of our own self-importance. That's what happened to the disciples. They argued with each other about who among them was the greatest.

But notice the lesson Jesus taught them. He used a little child as an example to illustrate to the disciples the very important principle of humility and service.

Mark's Gospel records Jesus' remarks this way:

> *. . . whosoever will be great among you, shall be your minister: and whosoever of you will be the chiefest, shall be servant of all.*
>
> *For even the Son of man came not to be ministered unto, but to minister, and to give his life a ransom for many.*
> *Mark 10:43-45*

If you don't try to promote yourself, if you just do God's work, witnessing to others and ministering to their needs, you will be great in the eyes of God. Once you begin to think you are something, that's when you become very little. The one who is the least among you shall be great. If you want to be great, be the servant of all.

Judge Not

> *And John answered and said, Master, we saw one casting out devils in thy name; and we forbad him, because he followeth not with us.*
> *Luke 9:49*

That sounds like a lot of churches and denominations today. Many of them think that anyone who isn't part of their little group can't be serving God and shouldn't be allowed to preach in their church. You'd be surprised how many churches won't let a Full Gospel minister preach in their sanctuary because "he's not one of us." That attitude is about as far from God as you can get. Never be guilty of judging or condemning other servants of God.

When you start thinking that you and your church are the best, you are in danger of losing your anointing, your power, and your effectiveness. In that case, some little church over by the railroad track with only a few members is greater in the eyes of God than your church. They keep themselves humble before God. They pray and win sinners to the Lord. They go out witnessing and pass out tracts. They have a burden for lost souls—and that's what makes a person or a church great.

Follow Thou Me

And Jesus said unto him, Forbid him not: for he that is not against us is for us.
Luke 9:50

Don't get your mind set on just one church. Be for all churches. You may not attend their church or believe entirely like they do, but give support through your prayers and testimony to all those who lift up the name of Jesus, who carry the Gospel to a lost and dying world. It is not our job as God's servants to judge other Christians. Like Jesus, our job is to do the will of Him Who sent us. Leave the judging to God. Don't concern yourself with how others are serving Him. As Jesus said to Peter, . . . *what is that to thee? follow thou me* (John 21:22).

You don't necessarily have to go to one certain church. You should go where you get fed—a place where you can receive God's Word and grow strong in the Lord to do His work, a place where you can flow with that particular ministry. If you can't flow with the ministry where you are now, then go to several other churches and try them. If you find that you can't flow anywhere, then you need to spend several days in prayer and get straightened out.

Some people float from one church to another. They've been to so many that they wouldn't know a good church when they saw it. They say, "Well, this church over here does some things I like and some things I don't like. I like the singing better at this church, but I like the preaching better over at that other church. I like the way the gifts of the Spirit are manifested in this church, but I like the pastor of that church better."

Don't fall into that trap. Find one church and get settled down. Start winning souls. Make your life count for God.

Remember What Spirit You Are Of

And it came to pass, when the time was come that he (Jesus) *should be received up, he stedfastly set his face to go to Jerusalem, and sent messengers before his face: and they went, and entered into a village of the Samaritans, to make ready for him. And they did not receive him, because his face was as though he would go to Jerusalem.*

And when his disciples James and John saw this, they said, Lord, wilt thou that we

> command fire to come down from heaven, and consume them, even as Elias did?
>
> But he turned, and rebuked them, and said, Ye know not what manner of spirit ye are of. For the Son of man is not come to destroy men's lives, but to save them. And they went to another village.
>
> Luke 9:51-56

James and John were very zealous for the Lord. They had good intentions, but they made one mistake: They forgot what kind of spirit they were of. When people didn't receive Jesus, they were ready to call down fire from heaven and consume them. "They won't receive You here, Jesus, so we'll just kill them."

It's wrong when people don't receive Jesus, but we shouldn't get indignant about it. We must guard against becoming ruthless in our zeal. Always remember, the Lord is compassionate. He rebuked the disciples for their attitude and reminded them that His mission wasn't to destroy, but to save.

> For God sent not his Son into the world to condemn the world; but that the world through him might be saved.
>
> John 3:17

Jesus wasn't sent to destroy. God isn't a murderer. Jesus said, *The thief cometh not, but for to steal, and to kill, and to destroy: I am come that they might have life, and that they might have it more abundantly* (John 10:10).

Jesus came to save, and that's what He sends us to do. It isn't our job to judge, condemn, or destroy. We must remember Who we serve and what His will is. He is *not willing that any should perish, but that all should come to repentance* (2 Pet. 3:9).

If James and John had known what kind of spirit was trying to get them, words like that wouldn't have come out of their mouths, or even into their heads. They forgot what kind of spirit they were of. Self got in the way. God doesn't think like humans do. These disciples were going through training. Later on, after they had learned a few things, God was able to write books through them.

You are getting educated, too. Knocking on doors to witness for Jesus is a good school for you. You'll soon find out what spirit you are of. Pray that God will live big in you. That's why I suggest that you pray before going out, so your spirit can be more like God's. You must keep your mind under subjection. If you don't pray and have power before you go out, your mind will take over. The natural part of your human personality will take control, and you'll get into conflict, confusion and strife. The Lord wants you to show His love to others. Regardless of how your message is received, you must operate in love. Never react in anger or resentment. Remember, *a soft answer turns away wrath.* (Prov. 15:1.)

When counseling soulwinning teams before they go out to witness, I always say, "After you have witnessed to a person, whether you win him to the Lord or not, always try to leave him in an atmosphere

Witnessing in Love

of love. If you don't, you haven't given Jesus much glory.''

If you will leave people in an atmosphere of love, the Lord can work with them after you've gone. Let your last words to that person or family be an expression of how much God loves them. If they reject you and your message of Jesus, don't react negatively—no matter what they may say or do. Before you leave, tell them that Jesus loves them and so do you. Always leave that atmosphere of love behind you because the Bible says faith works by love. (Gal. 5:6.)

Many times this is the trouble area in our witnessing. Like James and John, if people don't receive our message, we try to argue them into accepting it or bring curses down upon them if they don't. If they aren't interested in what we have to say, or if they are rude to us, we become offended or angry.

Then when we leave, that family will say, ''That's the trouble with these fellows. They are all alike. They have no business coming around our house, invading our property, trying to take over, trying to stuff religion down our throats. I just don't like their attitude!'' Just think what it will be like for the next person who comes along to witness to these people about the Lord.

Even if you don't win every person to Christ, if you will leave an atmosphere of love, God's Spirit can still move in their hearts. You have planted or watered the seed that was planted by someone else.

God will nurture that seed and tend it. He will cause it to grow and one day produce fruit in those lives.

Always remember, your greatest tool for witnessing is love. If you forget that, you are forgetting what kind of spirit you are of, because God is love. (1 John 4:16.)

Don't Give Up

In Luke 9 the Samaritans wouldn't receive Jesus, so James and John wanted to kill them. Jesus had to remind them of His mission—that He did not come to destroy, but to save.

Sometimes it's hard to keep our mission straight when we are rejected and abused. Some people would make great soulwinners except for one small thing—they can't stand rejection. Why should we act as though that was something unusual or unique? Why should we be surprised when we are sometimes rejected or offended? Even Jesus was rejected. How did He handle that rejection? What did He do? Did He give up and quit? No, He just told His disciples that He had come to save men's lives and souls, *and they went to another village* (Luke 9:56).

Even if you have been ordered off a person's property, the last words out your mouth should be that Jesus loves him. As you are walking off his property, say a prayer for him. Then just go to the next house.

Whatever you do, don't tuck your tail between your legs like a whipped dog and say, "Well, this

Witnessing in Love

isn't my ministry. I've had it. I'm through with this witnessing stuff. That fellow cursed me!"

Well, so what? Let him rave on. When you leave his house, bind up the cursing devil in him. Say, "You foul devil, I bind you in Jesus' name and command you to turn that man loose. He has a right to be saved so turn him loose!" Then go on to the next house and let the love of God come out of you. Don't let such experiences shake you up. If you do, you'll forget what kind of spirit you are of.

Paul reminds us: *For God hath not given us the spirit of fear; but of power, and of love, and of a sound mind* (2 Tim. 1:7). You haven't been defeated, not if you remain in control. Remember who you are and the God you serve. Remember whose Spirit is in you to guide and strengthen and empower you. Don't give up! Don't give in to discouragement or feelings of defeat!

Just do what Jesus did. Be calm. Go on to the next village. See if you can win some men in that village. If you don't, then go on to the next village, and the next, and the next.

My friend, there is no defeat for the child of God. Get defeat out of your mind. Don't entertain it. Don't even receive it. Slam the door in its face! You don't have to be defeated, regardless of people's reactions, because God hasn't given you a spirit of defeat, but a spirit of power and love and a sound mind. Just remember what spirit you are of.

Share The Good News

You can have anything from God that you want. God will give you all the power you need to do anything. Just don't forget what kind of spirit you are of. When you walk into a house to witness to someone who is lost, remember you are there for one reason: to save that person's life. You didn't come to cause him harm or to wish bad things on him, regardless of what he may say to you. Even if he rejects you, you are there to bless him and do him good.

Jesus was rejected, too. It makes men mad to be rejected. James and John said, "Well, we'll show them! We'll just pray fire out of heaven like Elijah did and consume them!" But they were wrong. We haven't been sent to destroy men's lives, to pray fire down from heaven to consume them. We've been sent to save men's lives.

Stop rebuking and criticizing men when you see them casting out devils in Jesus' name. Remember that everybody who isn't against us is for us. I wish denominational churches would remember that we are all part of the same Body of Christ. It isn't good to bar a person from speaking in a church just because he doesn't belong to a certain denomination. Or because he is a she! Regardless of a person's sex, race, age, or church membership, if he (or she) is anointed of God to minister to people's needs, he (or she) should be allowed to share what the Lord has done.

When you go out witnessing to others about Jesus, just know that your life is a blessing. Share that blessing with others and it will increase. The surest way to have more of any good thing in this life is to share it with others.

Every morning I wake up and say, "Lord, let me be a blessing to somebody today." Sometimes He sends me to spend the afternoon visiting cancer patients in the hospital. Before I go, I always pray and receive the blessing of the healing power of God upon me. I pray that it flow from me to them, in Jesus' name. Then when I go, I curse the cancers in Jesus' name, commanding them to die and disappear from their bodies.

There is no greater joy in life than to serve the Living God, sharing His blessings and love with those in need. Try it—you'll like it!

We Are Kings and Priests

The Revelation of Jesus Christ, which God gave unto him, to shew unto his servants things which must shortly come to pass; and he sent and signified it by his angel unto his servant John: who bare record of the word of God, and of the testimony of Jesus Christ, and of all things that he saw.

Blessed is he that readeth, and they that hear the words of this prophecy, and keep those things which are written therein: for the time is at hand.

John to the seven churches which are in Asia: Grace be unto you, and peace, from him

> *which is, and which was, and which is to come; and from the seven Spirits which are before his throne;*
>
> *And from Jesus Christ, who is the faithful witness, and the first begotten of the dead, and the prince of the kings of the earth. Unto him that loved us, and washed us from our sins in his own blood, and hath made us kings and priests unto God and his Father; to him be glory and dominion for ever and ever. Amen.*
> Revelation 1:1-6

Jesus was a faithful witness. He has now made you to be a faithful witness. He shed His blood so that you might become a king and a priest in Him. Because of what Jesus Christ has done for you, you are now second in power to God. Not even the devil has power over you!

When you were born again of the Spirit of God, you were restored to your rightful position, the position Adam enjoyed as lord of this earth. Like Adam, you have been given dominion over all the earth—including devils. But you have to know that you have such power and authority. Through what Christ did at Calvary, man has been restored to the state he was in before the fall of Adam.

Oh, if only man knew the dominion he holds! Because of the fall of Adam, the earth was cursed. Satan and his demons received from man the right to operate on this earth, to get into humans and to wreck their lives. But Jesus, by His substitutionary sacrifice, redeemed man from Satan's power. We were set free and restored to our rightful position as kings and priests in this earth!

Once you get born again by the Spirit of God, you don't have to take anything from Satan anymore. You are no longer living under the curse, because *Christ hath redeemed us from the curse of the law, being made a curse for us* (Gal. 3:13). You are no longer a sinner under condemnation; you have become the righteousness of God in Christ Jesus. (2 Cor. 5:21.) You are a king and a priest, the head and not the tail. You reign in this earth, not Satan. You should know who you are. You are free in Christ Jesus.

We Are Strong in the Lord

Behold, he cometh with clouds; and every eye shall see him, and they also which pierced him: and all kindreds of the earth shall wail because of him. Even so, Amen.

I am Alpha and Omega, the beginning and the ending, saith the Lord, which is, and which was, and which is to come, the Almighty.

I John, who also am your brother, and companion in tribulation, and in the kingdom and patience of Jesus Christ . . . .
Revelation 1:7-9

According to the Apostle John, Jesus is the Almighty and John is our brother and companion in tribulation. Well, that is what we are called to be, too—brothers and companions of those in tribulation. As you go to witness and minister to people, you can't give up on them. You have to stay with it until you get them set free. Death is right around the corner for people who give up. The devil always beats weak people into the ground. God doesn't want you to be weak; He wants you to be strong in the power of His might!

You may say, "But I don't feel strong. I'm not strong!" Then be determined like Elisha. Start walking the floor, confessing, "In Jesus' name, I'm not weak; I'm strong!" Do that long enough and God's power will make you strong. Give up and you won't get anything from God.

John also tells us that he is our brother and companion "in the kingdom and patience of Jesus Christ." Never say you don't have patience. Change your confession. Start confessing over and over every day: "I have patience in Jesus Christ." As you confess it, you will receive it. What you continue to confess about yourself with your mouth is what you will become.

> *I John . . . was in the isle that is called Patmos, for the word of God, and for the testimony of Jesus Christ.*
>
> *I was in the Spirit on the Lord's day, and heard behind me a great voice, as of a trumpet, saying, I am Alpha and Omega, the first and the last: and, What thou seest, write in a book . . . .*
>
> Revelation 1:9-11

The book John is referring to is the Bible, God's Word. It has already been spoken to John in the form of a vision and it has already been written by John. You've just been reading it.

Now it's up to you to believe it and obey it. You are to see yourself as a king and a priest in Christ Jesus. Devils are under your feet through Jesus Christ because He shed His blood for you. You aren't supposed to be dominated by them; they're to be dominated by you! Get your thinking straightened out according to God's Word and begin to see yourself as *more than a conqueror through Jesus Christ* (Rom. 8:37). You are called to be a brother and companion to the person who is beaten down by Satan. You are that person's brother in tribulation. Everybody wants to have friends who are successful, strong, and good; but God has called you to be a friend to those in tribulation—people who don't have anybody to help them.

Just Say the Word

To do that, you need a vision. *Without a vision,* the Bible says, *people perish* (Prov. 29:18). It's not enough just to go out and do your own thing. You may want to build a nice little church house on the corner and hold beautiful services on Sunday, a sweet little prayer meeting on Wednesday night, and a Sunday school social once a month. That's all very nice, but you can't win a city like that.

You have to spend some time in prayer and get some power down inside you. You have to be willing to walk the streets and get somebody saved, or go to a cancer ward and pray for the afflicted and dying. That is why you were made a king and a priest—to save lives and souls.

You Can Be A Soulwinner

Not long ago I went to the hospital to visit two cancer patients and a person in a mental ward. When I walked into the first room, I could sense the presence of Satan. The person who lay on the bed of affliction was in a terrible condition. It made me angry to see how the devil was tormenting her body with such a vile disease.

I walked to her bedside and said, "I curse this cancer, in Jesus' name. I command it to die and to cease being." As I began to pray, the healing power of God came; tears started to well up in her eyes, and she began to shake in bed.

I said, "You know the Lord is healing you, don't you?"

"Yes."

"You can even feel the Lord healing you, can't you?"

"Yes. I know He is."

I said, "Lie right there on your back and say, 'Thank You, Jesus, for healing me right now. I know You are healing me and I thank You for it.' "

She repeated it word for word. Then I told her, "Don't stop saying that. Say it today. Say it tonight. Say it tomorrow. Say it the day after."

The lady's sister was there in the room with us. She had come from out of town to give her sister encouragement. Then I said to her, "You'll be here with her, so make sure she says that over and over. Walk around her room saying, 'Thank You, Jesus, for healing my sister. The devil can't kill her. Thank You,

Jesus. I just praise You and worship You, Lord, for healing my sister right now.' "

That's how it works. You have to confess it. If you allow a person to lie flat on his back, waiting for other Christians to pray for him, you might as well order flowers for the funeral. To receive healing, a person has to do something himself to activate God's power. If he is so far gone that he can't do it for himself, then you or someone else has to do it for him. As a faithful witness and minister of Jesus Christ, you must initiate that action of faith. That is your responsibility.

You see, God responds to the words that come out our mouths, words from the Bible. When we start confessing the Scriptures, the Holy Spirit responds to our confession. He agrees with it; then He begins to manifest Himself and works to drive out the symptoms. The Holy Spirit of God works in response to the faith-filled confession of God's own Word. It's vitally important for you to know that. That's how miracles are released in people's lives.

When I prayed for Mike, the young man who needed deliverance from homosexuality, I knew what I was up against. Those devils had occupied a house—Mike's body—for sixteen years, and they weren't willing to give up easily. They thought they owned that house, and they didn't want to leave it.

Sometimes in cases like that, the demons will beg and plead, "Don't make me leave. He wants me here."

Jesus said the devil is a liar. You can't believe anything he says. When he says a person wants him there, it's a lie! Jesus is truth, and His name has power over all devils.

We must make a commitment to be a brother in tribulation to those in need, to be like John on the isle of Patmos, to pray for people and break the power of the devil over them so they can find the light of God and the freedom that Mike found.

I urge you to make that commitment right now. Pray this prayer of dedication with me:

"Heavenly Father, I come to You in Jesus' name and I ask You to come into my life totally and set me free from anything that is keeping me in bondage to Satan. I want to be free right now so I can serve You in power and authority.

"I promise You that, from this moment on, I will love You, worship You, and serve You. I commit myself, Lord, to be a faithful witness for You. I receive Your power to go forth and operate as a king and a priest in this world.

"Father, I covenant with You that I will be a brother in tribulation to those in need, that I will witness and minister to them Your salvation and restoration in the name of Jesus Christ.

"Thank You for the privilege of serving You and seeing lives transformed by Your power, in Jesus' name. Amen."

6
Pay the Price for Power

To be an effective witness for Jesus Christ, you have to be faithful. Faithfulness is the key to successful Christian living.

Every morning when you wake up, you should shake yourself and say, "I expect this to be the greatest day thus far in my life. Thank You, Jesus, for the opportunity to serve You today."

I've been doing this for years; and I can tell you, it works. I never get tired of serving the Lord, because the Holy Spirit doesn't get tired. Life never gets dull or boring or tedious to me, because I live by the Spirit of God. Every day of my life is dedicated to God and filled with His power.

You have to keep your body under subjection, keep it moving. You know, your body and your mind will lie to you. They will try to tell you, "You don't feel like going out and working for the Lord today. Why don't you do something else? You need a rest. Let somebody else do it. You've done your part. You're tired, so take it easy."

When you hear such thoughts, you just have to say, "Body, shut up! Glory to God, I'm going to win somebody to the Lord today. Now get up and get moving!"

The Apostle Paul knew this. He wrote in 1 Corinthians 9:27, *But I keep under my body, and bring it into subjection: lest that by any means, when I have preached to others, I myself should be a castaway.* Paul had learned that the proof of discipleship is not what you do on Sunday morning in a "high" type service. That is not where the power lies. According to Paul, the power is in the Gospel: *For I am not ashamed of the gospel of Christ: for it is the power of God . . .* (Rom. 1:16). The power of God is in the Gospel of Jesus Christ. But that power is developed through discipline. It is a way of life, a way of living, day in and day out.

Feelings Follow Action

When you start getting discouraged and start slacking off, you don't have God's power, you have your own power. God's power never gets tired or beaten down. God's power never has low days. I don't have low days. I'm "up" all day long, every day. My life is successful—full of love, full of power, and full of understanding—every day, because my life is full of God. I don't have any downtrodden, defeated days, because God doesn't have any.

That's the reason you have to act like you mean it. You have to make yourself get up, make yourself pray, make yourself go to church, make yourself open up your mouth and say, "Glory to God, this is the greatest day I've ever lived. Thank You, Lord, for making me a blessing to somebody today. Glory be to God forevermore!''

Don't wait until you feel like it. If you do, the devil will see to it that you never feel like it. You can't be subject to feelings. You have to make your feelings subject to you. No matter how you may feel, you have to take charge—start praising the Lord, start confessing with your mouth what His Word says, start putting your body into action. The feelings will have no choice but to follow.

People have asked me for years, ''Brother Norvel, don't you ever run down? Don't you ever feel defeated?'' I always say, ''No!'' You see, the Holy Ghost in me doesn't think like that, so neither do I. I can't afford to, and neither can you. You can't afford to let yourself get dull or lazy or down in the dumps. You have to keep yourself built up in God. If you don't, you'll lose your vision. The whole world will go to hell and you won't be able to do anything about it.

I don't care what kind of training you've had in the past, you can't let yourself get lax today. You may have been the best soulwinner in town three years ago, but what you did yesterday has nothing to do with today. You have to learn that. Today is a brand new day, and God is looking for you to win souls for Him *today!*

Be a blessing to somebody every day. Don't wait until you feel like it. Get into action and your feelings will get into line.

Pay the Price for Power

You have to pay the price to receive the power. I can't emphasize that too much. What kind of power? God's power. You can have it. Not just power to perform miracles—that's a part of it—but power to keep yourself built up in God and to do the things He wants you to do. If you don't keep yourself built up, you will never do anything for God. I can tell you that right now. As we have seen, this is a way of life, a way of living. You have to be like this all the time.

That's why many homes and marriages fall apart. Husbands and wives start fussing. They stop their prayer life. They don't spend time worshiping God in their home. They stop walking the floor hand in hand praying together. People get too busy to spend time in Bible reading and prayer and worship. Well, they need to get "unbusy."

Don't let your daily routine and the cares of the world rob you of what you are supposed to do for God. You have to pay the price of discipleship if you expect to have the power of God in your life. To be an effective witness, you have to pay the price to keep yourself built up in God.

What is the price you have to pay?

Wait for the Power

> *And, being assembled together with them,* (Jesus) *commanded them* (the disciples) *that they should not depart from Jerusalem, but wait for the promise of the Father, which, saith he, ye have heard of me.*

> *For John truly baptized with water; but ye shall be baptized with the Holy Ghost not many days hence.*
>
> *Acts 1:4,5*

Here the Lord Jesus was telling the disciples to wait in Jerusalem for the power to come. In the eighth verse He told them: *But ye shall receive power, after that the Holy Ghost is come upon you: and ye shall be witnesses unto me both in Jerusalem, and in all Judea, and in Samaria, and unto the uttermost part of the earth.*

Don't go out to witness without the power of God. Wait for the power to come. Wait for the promise. The promise is the power, the Holy Ghost, and He'll give you anything you want.

Always remember this, my friend: *The joy of the Lord is your strength* (Neh. 8:10). Once you lose your joy, you become a weakling. Without joy you won't do anything for God. You might make it to church on Sunday morning, but that's about all.

Now don't misunderstand. I'm not preaching against going to church. You should go to church regularly, and not just on Sunday morning either. I probably go to church more than anybody in America. Sometimes within three or four months, I have gone to church over ninety times. I probably go to church more than 365 times a year. Now that won't be every day. Sometimes I go to church three or four times in one day. I may go off on a trip and be in church 29 times in a three-week trip.

I never get tired of going to church. It's wonderful to be in the presence of God. But sometimes you need to get away and rest, to get alone with God.

When I'm not in church, I like to be alone with God, to keep my mind quiet and just rest in His holy presence. It's refreshing. We need those times of rest and refreshment. It does us so much good. God likes us to be with His children in church, but He also likes for us to get still and spend time alone with Him individually.

If you know how to adjust yourself, you'll never get tired of serving God, of winning people to Jesus. Your body might get tired, but you can rest your body for a while and come right back again. But if you want to rest, wait until you get home. It's hard to rest very much out on the field when you're winning souls.

Whatever you do, do it enthusiastically. In 1 Corinthians 10:31, we read, . . . *whatsoever ye do, do all to the glory of God.* Ecclesiastes 9:10 tells us, *Whatsoever thy hand findeth to do, do it with* (all) *thy might.*

We should go to church; we should join enthusiastically into the worship and praise. But just going to church isn't enough. Our Lord didn't call us to "go into all the world, and attend church." We have been saved, commissioned, and empowered to *go into all the world, and preach the gospel to every creature* (Mark 16:15). We are to do that joyfully and with enthusiasm.

The Lord tells us in 1 Peter 4:11, *If any man speak, let him speak as the oracles of God; if any man minister, let him do it as of the ability which God giveth: that God in all things may be glorified through Jesus Christ, to whom be praise and dominion for ever and ever. Amen.*

When you go out to witness, go in the power of the Holy Spirit. When you speak to people about Jesus, speak "as the oracles of God." When you minister to those in need, "do it as of the ability which God giveth."

Wait for the power of the Holy Spirit. Then go in that power and Spirit. You will be an effective witness for our Lord and God will be glorified.

Receiving the Power

When they therefore were come together, they asked of him, saying, Lord, wilt thou at this time restore again the kingdom to Israel?

And he said unto them, It is not for you to know the times or the seasons, which the Father hath put in his own power.

But ye shall receive power, after that the Holy Ghost is come upon you . . . .
Acts 1:6-8

How do you get the Holy Ghost to come upon you? The first step is to pray.

If you want to know the real truth about it, you can pray yourself into the Holy Ghost so that His holy presence just comes on you.

The Holy Ghost lives inside you. He talks to you from the inside. But there is a difference between having the Holy Spirit in you—talking to you, moving inside you, encouraging you to speak in tongues or operate in the gifts of the Spirit—and having the Holy Ghost come upon you. Having the Holy Ghost in you and having the Holy Ghost come upon you are not the same.

As a Christian you have the Holy Ghost living in you, but you can pray yourself into the holy presence of God so that the Spirit of the Lord will come upon you. It is a beautiful experience, but you have to pay the price to get it. Many times this will happen when you win a soul for God.

Suppose you bring a sinner to church and let him hear your pastor preach in the services. Usually when that person gets saved, you feel as though you got saved yourself. You are already saved, but God's holy presence is so clean, so pure, so powerful that you will experience it with the person being saved. God will let His Spirit come and overshadow you, giving you a blessing from heaven. And all of us need to be in God's holy presence as much as we can. It helps us think straight when God's holy presence comes on us.

And it helps when God's holy presence begins to come out of you too. It's just wonderful! You cry and laugh and weep and rejoice—all at the same time.

A couple of times in my life the Lord has blessed me so much, I had to ask Him to stop. I said, "Lord, if You don't stop, I'm not going to be able to do my work." Once that happened, and it lasted for three days! I would go to work and just sit behind my desk. It would be all I could do to just sit there and take it.

Pay the Price for Power

When the phone would ring, it sounded way off some place. Someone would answer it and say, "Telephone, Mr. Hayes." I would take the receiver, but could hardly talk.

You can get so far in God's holy presence that you couldn't care less about the world and the things going on around you. You just want to let the world go by, because you are enjoying God's power so much.

Purpose of the Power

> *But ye shall receive power, after that the Holy Ghost is come upon you: and ye shall be witnesses unto me both in Jerusalem, and in all Judea, and in Samaria, and unto the uttermost part of the earth.*
>
> *Acts 1:8*

If you will pray yourself into the presence of God, the Spirit of God will come upon you. You will be the same kind of witness in Paris, France, that you would be in Tulsa, Oklahoma, because you don't ever change.

You may say, "Well, I don't see how that could be. I don't speak French. I couldn't talk to those people in Paris."

But you would be so enthused that you would find an interpreter to take with you. If he wasn't saved, he would be before long. If you will pray until the Spirit of the Lord comes upon you, you will have power to witness to anyone anywhere. When the power of God is upon you, it doesn't make any difference where you are, who you are witnessing to, or what their problem is. When the power of God is on you, you can't see anything but victory!

That is the purpose of receiving the power of the Holy Spirit. That is what the power of the Spirit is for: to empower us to be effective witnesses of Jesus Christ. The Holy Spirit was given by Jesus to empower His disciples to go out and win souls to Him.

Jesus said that He came *to seek and to save that which was lost* (Luke 19:10). And when He went back to heaven to sit at the right hand of God the Father, He passed that job on to us, His disciples. But He didn't leave us without the authority and power to do the job. That authority and power came when He sent the Holy Spirit. That's the purpose of the power—to win souls. Now our job is to go into all the world and use that power.

Be Filled with the Spirit

You may be sitting there thinking, *Well, I don't know, Brother Norvel. I don't feel much like witnessing to the uttermost part of the earth.*

Well, you can feel like it if you'll pray. There's nothing wrong with you. You're just lazy. You need to put action first and feelings second. If you will set yourself to pray yourself into the holy presence of God, you'll start feeling like that. It all depends upon the condition of your spirit inside you. You can do anything for God that I can do, but you can't do it unless your spirit is in the right kind of condition. You can't do it, and you won't do it. Unless you keep your spirit in the right kind of condition—that means full of strength, full of love, and full of power—you will never do anything of value for the Lord. You have to keep your spirit full of the Holy Spirit, His power, and His love.

How do you keep your spirit full? First of all, you worship God. You tell Jesus every day that you love Him. The easy way to do that is by being baptized in the Spirit. But you can witness effectively even if you never get baptized in the Holy Ghost.

How do Christians witness if they aren't baptized in the Holy Spirit? Where do they get the power? Most Baptists are better witnesses for Christ than most Pentecostals. How can they be? I'll tell you how. Baptists pray. How do they pray? In English. It pays to pray in English, if you don't know how to pray in tongues. You can get on the floor and pray in English and the Spirit of God will come upon you. You can pray yourself into the holy presence of God by praying in English, just the same as you can by praying in tongues. It takes longer and it isn't quite as powerful, but it can be done.

If you are born again by the Spirit of God, all sin has left you regardless of your denomination. When you earnestly pray in English, the Spirit of God will come upon you and start blessing you; then you'll want to go out and win somebody for God. And you'll have enough power to do it!

But let me pass something on to you. You can do more with the baptism of the Holy Ghost. Now getting baptized in the Holy Ghost won't make you more of a child of God, but it will give you more power. Witnessing becomes easier. Praying yourself into the presence of God is easier and quicker if you can pray in tongues instead of English. I don't have to get flat on the floor and pray in English for two or three hours to get the power of God. All I have to do now is just keep my spirit built up continually by speaking in tongues. That way I don't ever get down or discouraged.

If I feel myself getting weak and discouraged, I pray in tongues more. But I don't ever feel weakness or discouragement to any degree. I haven't had that for years, because I try to keep myself praying in tongues every day. I know how to keep my spirit built up at a level where I don't allow myself to get beaten down. I don't want to lose my vision for lost people. I don't want to get where I no longer care about witnessing to others.

"Full Gospel" Is Full Power

If you let yourself get down like that, it's your own fault. Paul explains to us in his writings exactly what to do. In 1 Corinthians 14:4 he tells us, *He that speaketh in an unknown tongue edifieth himself.*

You see, praying in tongues edifies a person. The word *edify* means "to build up." If you get baptized in the Holy Ghost and know what to do to keep yourself built up, then you can make a better soulwinner because you'll keep your spirit stronger.

Pay the Price for Power

You won't just win souls; you will also pray for the sick and cast out devils, as Jesus talked about in Mark 16:17,18.

The baptism of the Holy Ghost is "full Gospel." Until you get baptized in the Holy Ghost, you can win souls for God and keep yourself built up to a degree, but you are only involved in a "part Gospel." You are involved in the best part, to be sure. Winning souls for God is the heart of the Gospel.

A person only knows what he has been taught. Usually before a person gets baptized in the Holy Ghost, his spirit is closed to things he hasn't been taught. After being baptized in the Holy Ghost, his spirit opens up to be more receptive to God's Word. He responds better to God's Word and his spirit is more open to the things of God.

Probably before you got baptized in the Holy Ghost you wanted to argue about the Bible. You should never do that. There is no use in arguing about it because the Bible doesn't change. You might as well make up your mind that everything in the New Testament is true. You might as well quit arguing against it and just receive it. I don't care if it is casting out devils, speaking in tongues, or laying hands on the sick—if it's in God's Word, it's true. You might as well get started doing it because we've been hanging on to tradition and lying in the lap of laziness too long.

God wants every pastor to obey the Bible from Genesis through Revelation. Until they do, they will be ignorant, and so will their congregations because a congregation usually believes what the pastor believes.

People can only receive from God what they are taught to believe for. Jesus told those who came to Him for healing, *According to your faith be it unto you* (Matt. 9:29). A person will receive no more from God than what he has faith to receive. Many times his faith depends upon what he has been taught. If he hasn't been taught to believe that by the stripes of Jesus he is healed, then he can't receive his healing.

Baptists believe in free salvation by grace. They teach it. They experience it. They witness to others about it. But generally Baptists don't believe or teach that it's God's will to heal everybody. How can they receive something if they don't know whether it's God's will for them to have it?

Baptists generally don't lay hands on the sick or cast out devils. Because they don't preach or practice these things, they don't receive miraculous healings or see their loved ones delivered from demon possession by the power of God working through His servants. It's really very simple: A person receives from God what he has been taught to receive.

There are some 37,000 churches in the Southern Baptist Convention. A person can get saved in any one of those churches, and thousands of people are saved every year. Baptists are unsurpassed when it comes to getting people saved. That's good and commendable. But the record of cripples getting healed in Baptist churches is absolutely zero.

God is pleased that Baptists are getting people saved, but He also wants people healed and set free. Why aren't Baptists doing that in their churches? Because they aren't taught to do that.

If Jesus Christ walked into the First Baptist Church of any city in America on Sunday morning, He would empty the wheelchairs, heal every blind eye, and open every deaf ear. He would lay His hands on cancerous bodies and smite those afflictions.

That's what we are supposed to be doing. When we do it, Jesus has enough power in Him to get the job done. You and I have to operate by faith in God's Word. We have to motivate people to believe for healing. People receive according to their faith. Jesus said so. Their believing plays a role. But for them to have faith, they must be taught faith.

The Bible says God gave His Spirit to Jesus without measure. (John 3:34.) But you and I receive it with measure. What is that measure? The New Testament. You and I receive the Spirit according to our faith in God's Word. We have to be Bible believers. We have to study the Bible and find out what it says. We have to get God's Word inside us. With the Word lodged inside your spirit, you can open your mouth and boldly proclaim the Word of God. Then the Spirit of God will confirm that Word. He does what you say and what you believe, if it's scriptural.

You see, the Bible teaches that the Spirit of God agrees with the Word, and that's all He agrees with.

You and I are living in the dispensation of grace, mercy, and faith. Faith in what? Faith in the Bible. When you start having faith in God's Word and start speaking out God's Word, the Spirit of God will confirm that Word that comes out of you. God wants you to spend time reading the Bible and praying because those are two main ingredients in spiritual power.

The full Gospel produces full power. If you aren't going to spend time reading the Bible and praying, you might as well start driving a truck, because you aren't going to get anything done for God. You are just going to be floating along, wondering why things don't happen. Things happen because you make them happen. As long as you wonder why nothing is happening, nothing is going to happen. You have to get in agreement with the Bible. When you agree with God's Word, His Spirit will agree with you. Then as you speak forth that Word in faith and power, the Holy Spirit will go forth and cause the thing you say to come to pass.

If you haven't been doing that, then get started. When you do, you won't have any more weak, beaten-down days. Your life will start blossoming like a flower in springtime, and you'll be like that every day. The sweet fragrance of God will flow out from you every day to a lost and dying world.

Oh, the blessed Word of God! The Gospel of Jesus Christ never loses its flavor. The sweet holy presence of God wants to work for you and with you every day of your life. The Holy Spirit has everything you need. Being baptized in the Holy Ghost provides you access to all the wisdom and power of God Almighty Himself.

Edify Yourself With Tongues

When Jesus was taken up from the disciples, He told them not to leave Jerusalem until they had received the promise. (Acts 1:4,5). The promise of what? The promise of the Holy Spirit—the promise of power, the promise of tongues.

> *Then returned they unto Jerusalem from the mount called Olivet, which is from Jerusalem a sabbath day's journey.*
>
> *And when they were come in, they went up into an upper room, where abode both Peter, and James, and John, and Andrew, Philip, and Thomas, Bartholomew, and Matthew, James the son of Alphaeus, and Simon Zelotes, and Judas the brother of James.*
>
> *These all continued with one accord in prayer and supplication, with the women, and Mary the mother of Jesus, and with his brethren.*
>
> Acts 1:12-14

These all continued with one accord in prayer. All of them thought alike. They all prayed. That's the opposite of some of them being lazy and letting the rest of the church pray for them. They stayed there for ten days and nights like that in continual prayer and supplication, in one accord. And what was the result?

> *And when the day of Pentecost was fully come, they were all with one accord in one place.*
>
> *And suddenly there came a sound from heaven as of a rushing mighty wind, and it filled all the house where they were sitting.*
>
> *And there appeared unto them cloven tongues like as of fire, and it sat upon each of them.*
>
> *And they were all filled with the Holy Ghost, and began to speak with other tongues, as the Spirit gave them utterance.*
>
> Acts 2:1-4

If you will study the twelfth through the fourteenth chapters of 1 Corinthians, you will see what the Apostle Paul says about the importance of tongues and praying in tongues. In 1 Corinthians 14:18, he said, *I thank my God, I speak with tongues more than ye all.* Now if Paul spoke in tongues more than the entire Corinthian church, he must have spoken in tongues nearly all the time! That must have been about all he did, because those Corinthians spoke in tongues so much they had to be reprimanded about it. They just went wild with it. Paul had to write them a letter and tell them to try to keep things straight, to keep their worship services orderly. Yet Paul says, "I thank God, I speak in tongues more than you all!"

Well, I'm going to tell you right now that if you will spend time during the day, just a few times each day, speaking in tongues, your spirit won't get beaten down. It will stay built up. The Bible says, *He that speaketh in an unknown tongue edifieth himself* (1 Cor. 14:4). If you'll spend the time to speak in tongues, it will keep your spirit up so you will have the strength you need to witness.

Every morning when you first wake up, tell the Lord that you love Him. Raise up your hands and begin to worship Him. Then start speaking in tongues. Pray in tongues while you are getting dressed, while you are driving to work. Speak in tongues several times during the day and your spirit will just stay at a high level of strength. After a while people will begin to look at you and ask, "Don't you ever get beaten down? Don't you ever feel sad? Don't you ever get tired? Don't you ever feel like throwing up your hands and quitting?"

I don't ever get that way, and I'm not going to! The only reason you get that way is because you haven't been reading the Bible enough, or praying enough, or speaking in tongues enough.

Ye Shall Receive Power

You see, God's power is available for everybody—every individual in every church in America. God has enough power for every church and every church member in the whole world. This coming Sunday morning the power of God wants to come into every Christian church to save the lost, heal the sick, minister to the brokenhearted, and set the captives free. That's what Jesus came to do. In Luke 4:18,19 we read where Jesus stood up in church and said:

> *The Spirit of the Lord is upon me, because he hath anointed me to preach the gospel to the poor; he hath sent me to heal the brokenhearted, to preach deliverance to the captives, and recovering of sight to the blind, to set at liberty them that are bruised,*
>
> *To preach the acceptable year of the Lord.*

Well, has Jesus' ministry changed? No. The Church of Jesus Christ was established to carry out that ministry. And there is power enough to accomplish it. If it isn't being done, whose fault is it? It's the Church's fault.

The power of God is available to you to accomplish the mission God has given you. You can receive that power—if you will pay the price in Bible reading, prayer, and edification.

What kind of power? Power to reach out to a lost and dying world, power of compassion, power of strength, power of authority over devils who try to wreck the human race.

No devil has power over you. Jesus Himself has put all devils under the soles of your feet. You don't have to listen to the devil. You're not serving him. You're serving the Most High God. You have His Spirit inside you; and if you'll let Him have His way, He'll make you full of love and full of power.

Pay the price and you can have the power. Anybody can. It isn't for just a few people. Anyone who will pay the price can have it.

Pay the Price for Power

Pay the price. Receive the power. Be a witness and a minister for Jesus Christ. A lost and dying world is waiting for someone to bring them deliverance. Be that someone. Go into all the world and preach the Good News to every creature.

7
Practical Suggestions for Effective Witnessing
by
Jimmy Maynor

Successful witnessing is simply sharing Christ in the power of the Holy Spirit and leaving the results to God. We can't save anybody. Jesus didn't command us to go out and save anybody. He commanded us to go out and witness to others, to take the Good News of the Gospel to every creature. The Bible says that Peter was told to take certain words to Cornelius and his household whereby they could be saved. (Acts 10.) That's what we are called to do.

Now you can learn how to do that in an easy, pleasing, and effective way. It's easy to witness, if you know how. If it's done right, witnessing can be both pleasant and effective.

Let's begin by learning how to make a successful home visit. Now I've witnessed quite a bit in streets and in some areas that can be dangerous. We should not be afraid to witness anywhere, even in the worst ghetto districts of our large cities. I have done that, and still do; and because of the power and presence of God's Holy Spirit, I am not afraid. You shouldn't worry and be concerned about your life when witnessing in such areas. You should know that God is in control and that no weapon formed against you shall prosper. (Is. 54:17.)

There are many places you can't go to witness when you are afraid. If you walk up to people who are selling dope on the street or in some dark alley, they know when you are afraid. That kind of people sense fear. The demons in them can sense the fear in you. But if you'll approach them without fear, they won't bother you. Don't go to places like that if you are afraid. Wait until you have built up your confidence through experience. Begin to develop your confidence by witnessing to people in safe neighborhoods in their own homes.

The reason most people don't witness is because they are afraid. You have to deal with fear. The best way to get over that fear is by witnessing house to house because there is no danger to you there. Some people might be rude and slam the door in your face once in a while, but there is no real danger.

How to Witness in the Home

How do you go about witnessing to people in their homes? Let's talk about that.

Be Prepared

The first step in witnessing effectively in the home is to be prepared before you go. Before I visit a person in his home, if at all possible I like to have

Practical Suggestions for Effective Witnessing

some information about him. The more you know about a person the better able you are to witness to him about his particular situation or need. For instance, in addition to his name and address, I like to know whether he is an alcoholic or a drug addict, if he has a marriage or family or financial problem, what kind of health he is in, etc.

Then I like to pray and intercede for that person before I call on him. If he is an alcoholic, I want to take an ex-alcoholic with me. If he is a drug addict, I want to take an ex-drug addict with me. I always want someone with me who has experienced the same problems that person is experiencing. That gives me added strength and support as I deal with him on the level of his need. That's where we reach people for Christ, on the level of their needs.

Let's suppose that I am going out witnessing and that I am taking with me two people, Libby Chapman and Dick Rogers. Let's say that we are going to visit a man named George. Now I don't want to go out there on a hit-or-miss basis; I want to be effective. If I have that person's name on a card, then I know I can be more effective because I can call him by his name. I go armed with his name and any other information I can gather about him; I am supported by two other people to assist me; and I go backed by prayer and in the power of the Holy Spirit. When I go out to witness, I go prepared.

Be Brief

I knock on George's door. When he opens it, I say, "Are you George Brown? My name is Jimmy

Maynor. This is Libby Chapman and Dick Rogers. We're from Such-and-Such Church and we're out visiting this afternoon.''

Don't ever tell people that you are ''witnessing.'' You don't want to frighten them by saying that. Use the word ''visiting.''

Then I say, ''May we come in for just a few minutes?'' Now it is very important to say ''for a few minutes,'' because people are busy. They aren't really interested in anybody coming in their home and taking up their valuable time. So it's very important that you say, ''May we come in for a **few** minutes?''

When you get inside, stick to what you said—stay only a few minutes. I have sent out some witnessing teams that got into people's homes and stayed half a day. I could go out and win eight or ten people while they were visiting in one home. You don't need to stay for two hours. Go in, get those people saved, then go somewhere else and get other people saved.

Most of the time you should try to limit your visit to about fifteen or twenty minutes. If the person is really receptive and you can see that he isn't in any hurry, you might stay a little longer, maybe thirty minutes—but no longer. That is plenty of time to stay in one house.

Occasionally I have run into a person who has a lot of questions and objections, and I had to deal with those. The way to deal with objections is with the Word of God.

Practical Suggestions for Effective Witnessing

The person may say, "Well, I believe this . . ."

You say, "But the Word of God says . . ."

"I believe so and so."

"But the Word of God says such and such."

Don't think that you have to memorize all the Scriptures before you can go witnessing. I know a man who takes a tract and reads it, word for word, to the person he is witnessing to. He gets hundreds of people saved every year. You can go out witnessing *today* and you can be effective *today*. But you do need to develop some skills. You need to learn key scriptures that will help you answer the questions people might ask. This will help you start where you are and build a foundation for witnessing. Finally, you'll reach the place where you'll have all the right answers for all the questions that people might ask.

Take Others With You

When I make a home visit, I like to take two people with me. After over twenty years of witnessing experience, I have learned that this is best. I usually like to have a man and a woman with me.

I have all kinds of people who come up to me and say, "Oh, Jimmy, that's not the Bible way. The Bible says they went out in twos." Well, let me tell you something: Whatever works for you is what you ought to do. Whatever works is best. The way that works best for me in witnessing house to house is a team of three—me, another man, and a woman.

For witnessing on the street, two people make a good team. That's all you need. Two is sufficient for street witnessing, but in home witnessing you are going to be more effective with a team of three. I'll show you why.

Sooner or later you are going to run into trouble. The devil isn't going to sit around and let you spoil his house without causing trouble. When he does, you need some help. The people going with me are there to help me. I'm going to do the witnessing; they are going to help me. They know what their job is. You see, I train my people. They know what they are to do. Their job is not to do the actual witnessing; that's my job.

Three people can't witness to one person at the same time. Only one can do the witnessing. I've seen people who could have been saved but weren't because three people were trying to talk to them at once. There was nothing but confusion. Don't do that. Let one person do the talking. One person does the witnessing; the other two are there to help.

Get Close to the Person

You can't witness effectively to a person if you are sitting across the room from him. You can lead people to the Lord this way, but it is much more difficult to do.

When I talk to a person, I want to sit right beside him. As I share God's Word with him, I don't want him to just take for granted what I am saying. I want him to be able to see for himself **in the Bible** what I am talking about. I tell people, "I know you aren't interested in what I have to say. You are interested in what the Word of God has to say." I want that

Practical Suggestions for Effective Witnessing

person to be able to read with me the scriptures which I point out to him. How can I do that if he is on the other side of the room? I can't.

If you just read or quote scriptures to people, generally you will lose about fifty percent of the people you witness to.

Well, how do I get people to sit where I want them to? I want to teach you how to do that. In most homes—not every home, but most—there will be a couch and two chairs in the living room.

Suppose I am visiting with George and I want him to sit beside me. To get him to do that, I tell the people who are with me that as soon as we walk into the room they are to fill up the two empty chairs. I don't wait around and let George sit down in one of those chairs across from me. My people are trained to head straight for those two chairs. That way there is no place left for George to sit but with me on the couch.

You say, "Does that work?" Absolutely. That is one reason why I like to have two people with me, to help set the scene so that I can get close enough to the person to deal with him and share God's Word with him.

Keep His Attention

The reason I like to have both a man and a woman with me is because there are situations that only a man can handle, and there are situations that only a woman can handle. When you go into a home, there will be obstacles to overcome. One of these obstacles is children. In about thirty to forty percent of the homes I visit, children are a problem in witnessing.

If I have a woman with me, she can take care of the children. If the kids start acting up, that woman knows what to do. She will go over and play with them, entertain them, and keep them from interrupting my presentation.

If I am witnessing to George and his wife on the couch and the little boy starts causing a ruckus, or the baby starts crying, the woman with me is trained to immediately go into action. She will play with that little boy or take care of the baby. If the mother has to get up and care for the baby herself, or if the baby keeps on crying, then it is hard to witness. But if the woman with me takes care of that situation, then the mother is free for me to continue to witness to her.

The lady with me can also be a help if I'm witnessing to someone and a neighbor drops in for a mid-morning cup of coffee. My lady assistant would introduce herself and draw that person away so that she doesn't interrupt my witnessing.

The man is there to do exactly the same thing with the men and boys of the house and neighborhood. He can help corral kids, talk to teenagers, or keep other men from interfering while I witness to the man of the house. You see, in witnessing you have to be as wise as a serpent and as harmless as a dove. You have to know that you are out there for only one reason: to win someone to Jesus. You have to be determined that you aren't going to let anything interfere with your witness.

Practical Suggestions for Effective Witnessing

You see, the devil will do anything and use anything to create a disturbance, to distract the person's attention from your message. You need to be prepared for anything Satan might try. One obstacle you may have to overcome is the person's dog. Many times while I'm witnessing, everything will go along fine as long as I'm talking about something unrelated to the Gospel. But the instant I start to talk about Jesus, that person's dog will go into a rage, and start barking or snarling. I have even had them to attack me and bite me on the leg.

You need to understand that the devil will use children, dogs, and other things to try to break your witness. You must be prepared for whatever may happen, so you can keep the person's attention long enough to lead him to the Lord.

Be Attractive

When you go out to witness to people, be careful to present a good impression of yourself and your Lord. You should be neat, clean, well-groomed, pleasant, and personable. Be careful not to offend people by your manner, attitude, personal appearance, or habits.

One practical piece of advice is to watch your breath. Take some kind of breath mints along. You might not think that you have bad breath, but don't take any chances. It's hard to sit right next to someone and win them to the Lord if your breath knocks them down. Don't take chances with that person's eternal destiny. Remember, we're playing to win.

If you have ever done any selling, you know that you have to sell yourself before you can sell your product. You'll never get inside a house unless you present yourself right. You have to be friendly, courteous, neat, and attractive. You can't be pushy. If you are, you will never get any place.

When you go out to witness, dress (if possible and reasonable) like the people to whom you are going. Paul said, *I am made all things to all men, that I might by all means save some* (1 Cor. 9:22). In other words, Paul put himself on the level of the person to whom he was witnessing. So should you. Don't talk over his head or beneath his intelligence. Don't overdress or underdress. Just be sure that you are neat, clean, and attractive.

Bind the Devil

Before my team goes out to witness, we pray. We break the power of the devil over the people we are going to see. If you will pray before you go and bind Satan from interfering, you will tear down a lot of obstacles that would hinder you.

Now I don't have the space to go into all the kinds of hindrances you will encounter; but if you will spend the time it takes in prayer before you go out, your witnessing will be much more effective and fruitful. If you have set aside three hours for witnessing, it would be better to spend thirty to sixty minutes in prayer and the rest of the time in actual witnessing than it would to spend the whole three hours in witnessing without prayer. You will actually win more souls if you will spend more time in prayer before you go.

Practical Suggestions for Effective Witnessing

You can stop the devil in a lot of things, and it's better to stop him before you go than it is to go out and have to deal with him there. That's the reason I like to know something about the people I am going to see. I'm more effective if I can pray for them before I go. I can prepare myself in prayer before I meet them and pray for them and their particular needs. I can bind Satan from interfering with my witness to that need.

Before we enter a house, we pray. We bind the power of the devil. We bind up the angry spirits and the cursing spirits. I don't let the devil run rampant in the houses where I go to witness. I just don't permit it. What you permit, God will permit. What you do not allow, God will not allow. The Bible says that whatever you bind on earth will be bound in heaven and whatever you loose on earth will be loosed in heaven. (Matt. 18:18.) Before you go out to witness, you have to do some binding.

Be Observant

If you go to witness in the house of a person you don't know, be observant. Study the house and yard so you can know more about the person you have come to see.

If I go up to a house and see a fishing boat parked in the yard, I know the man likes to fish. Therefore, I can talk to him about fishing.

You say, "I didn't know you were going to talk about fishing."

Oh, yes. I want to talk to that man about whatever it is that interests him. Until I get him relaxed, I am going to talk about his interests. Then when I get him relaxed, I can just move right into my witnessing and lead him to the Lord Jesus.

When I go to a house, I look around. Are there toys or swings in the yard? Is there a nice little flower garden? This type of thing tells me about the family, whether there are children in the family and their approximate ages, what the lady of the house is interested in, what is important to them.

Be observant. Learn all you can about that family before you go in to talk with them. Then begin by talking about their interests.

Know How to Present Your Product

When you go up to a house and ring the doorbell, don't stand right in the door. Ring the bell, then step back a little so you won't seem pushy. When the person comes to the door, be friendly. Immediately introduce yourself and your team.

If you do it right, you'll get in at least seven out of ten homes. But don't be pushy. If they don't allow you in, don't try to force your way in. In the years that I have been witnessing, I have learned some things. Christians who have gone before me have made it harder for me to witness to people because they have been too pushy. You can't cram Jesus down people's throats. Remember that. You have to witness in an easy, relaxed, pleasant way.

Witnessing in homes is not like witnessing on the streets. You can't go up to people and tell them that they are going to hell if they don't get saved. That won't work. In street witnessing you are dealing

Practical Suggestions for Effective Witnessing

with hard people and that requires hard measures. You don't soft-soap prostitutes, pimps, dopeheads, and drunks. You have to be as tough as they are if you are ever to reach that kind. But we are not talking about that type of witnessing here. In this study we are primarily concerned with the beginning stage of witnessing, which is witnessing to people in their own homes.

In a house visit you must remember that you are a guest in that person's home. You must act like one. You must be friendly, courteous, and mannerly.

But you must also have a plan. A good salesman always has a plan; he knows how he is going to present his product. He may alter his presentation a little, depending upon the person or the situation; but generally he sticks pretty close to his prepared plan. If you are going to be an effective soulwinner, you must stick to your plan, too. At times the Holy Ghost will lead you another way and change your plans. But basically you want to stick to what you have prepared.

To illustrate, let's imagine that my team and I have gained entrance into George's home. My teammates have sat down in the two chairs, leaving me to sit beside George on the couch. Now what do I say to him? How do I open the conversation?

Suppose that when we approached the house, I saw a fishing boat in the yard and a set of golf clubs in the garage. That means George is interested in fishing and playing golf. I might make a comment like this, "You know, it's really nice today, isn't it?

Sure would be a good day to go fishing, wouldn't it? Are you a fisherman?" This gives me a chance to get him talking about what he likes.

Or I might say, "Well, how do you like this beautiful fall weather? This is really good golfing weather, isn't it?" You see, I strike up a conversation with him and I talk about something that interests him. I don't do all the talking; I let him talk some. While he is talking, I listen. I let him know that I'm interested in what he has to say.

When you talk to a person, you want him to be interested in what you are saying, don't you? Well then, when he talks to you, be interested in what he is saying. After a minute or two of talking about the weather or fishing or golfing or whatever, that person will be more relaxed. He or she will be getting used to you, feeling at ease with you.

When I introduced myself to this man, he told me that his name was George Brown. After talking with him for a few minutes, I say, 'Would it be all right, Mr. Brown, if I just called you George?" You have to be led of the Spirit to do this, but I have found that I witness better if I get on a first-name basis with the person. I tell him that my name is Jimmy and ask if it would be all right if I called him by his first name.

After I have talked to him about these other things for a while, I take out my New Testament. Now when you go to witness house to house, never take a big Bible with you. A big Bible is a hindrance. If you walk up the sidewalk with a big Bible under your arm, the person may look out the window and see

Practical Suggestions for Effective Witnessing

you coming. He immediately thinks you will try to come in and stay all day. So he locks the door or just refuses to answer it.

Keep your weapon concealed. Put it someplace where it isn't too obvious. You can bring it into action when you need it.

So we're sitting on the couch, George and I. We have finished talking about golfing and fishing. I look over at George and I say, "George, what I really want to talk to you about today is this: Are you prepared for eternity?"

I ask this in a loving kind of voice, a meek voice, a very low-keyed voice.

"Are you prepared for eternity? What would happen to you if you died tonight? Would you go to heaven?"

Most of the time, the person will answer, "No, I don't think I would."

So then I say, "That's the reason the Lord Jesus sent me here today. The Bible says the steps of a good man are ordered by the Lord. It's no accident that I'm here at your home today. The Lord Jesus has sent me here to share with you how you can be sure that you will go to heaven when you die."

Then I go into my testimony. I take about three minutes and give him my own personal testimony of what the Lord has done for me. I tell him what my life was like before I received Christ and what it's like now, since I have made Him my Lord and Savior.

I don't always say the same thing. Sometimes I give a testimony of healing or of what God has done in my life—how He grew me from a midget to a full-grown, normal man. I don't always do this. Basically I'm just led by the Spirit.

A testimony should be something that God has done for you—a miracle He worked for you, what your life was like before you received Christ, how you came to find Christ as your personal Savior, how He has helped you since you have been a Christian.

I share that testimony, then I pull out my New Testament and say, "I just want to show you a few steps in the Bible that will make it clear to you how you too can be saved and know that you are going to heaven."

Then I share with him the plan of salvation, having him follow in the Bible the scriptures I use. Then when I have done that, I ask him, "Now wouldn't you like to accept Jesus Christ as your Lord and Savior right now? Wouldn't you like to know that your sins are forgiven and that you are going to spend eternity in heaven with Jesus? If you would, just bow your head and repeat this prayer after me." Then I lead him in the sinner's prayer.

Now I know this works. It works for me. It doesn't matter what method you may use. Use whatever works best for you. But I have won thousands of people to the Lord with my little New Testament and that simple plan. It isn't complicated. It's very simple, but it works. It works because the Gospel of Jesus Christ is the power of God unto salvation. (Rom 1:16.)

8
Questions and Answers on Effective Witnessing

The following is a question and answer session led by Norvel Hayes, Jimmy Maynor, and Angelo Mitropoulos at the conclusion of a soulwinning seminar held in Tulsa, Oklahoma.

Q. Do you ever have any trouble getting people to let you into their homes?

Jimmy: Usually not. As we have said, when you go out to witness you have to sell yourself before you can get in to talk about Jesus.

When you go up to a house, if both the screen door and the inside door are closed, but the screen door is unlocked, open it and knock on the door. Don't stand too close to the door, but keep the screen door open with your foot. That way, when the person open the inside door, you'll be looking at him or her, eyeball to eyeball.

If the screen door is locked, and the person doesn't open it, then you'll have to talk to him through the screen. This makes it harder, but you can still get in if you are friendly—not pushy, but friendly.

You Can Be A Soulwinner

You will find that generally people who live in average or lower income areas will be more inclined to open their doors to you than those in the higher income areas. Sometimes it seems that the upper-crust people—those who have everything they need—are rather snobbish. If you go to witness in a high income area, you will find it more difficult to get people to let you into their homes.

Norvel: Let me add something to that, Jimmy. When I gave my life to Jesus, I was making $5,000 a week. God kept dealing with me to give my life to Him, but I wouldn't do it because I had four Cadillacs in my driveway and thought I didn't need anything from anybody.

I was a successful businessman in my twenties. My pastor had his doctorate, and my assistant pastor was a theologian with several seminary degrees. When you have doctors and lawyers as your friends, you don't think you need anything.

I can relate to people on all levels because I have been there myself. I was the kind of fellow who could do anything. I was born and raised in a sharecropper family in Tennessee. I know what it is to work for twenty-five cents a day. I used to work for that as a youngster. But I worked real hard and by the time I was in my twenties, I was a financial success. Everything I had was paid for. I know what it is to be with good, honest, down-to-earth people who don't make much money. I know what it is to be middle class. I also know what it is to have millionaire friends and be part of the country club set. So let me pass on a piece of advice.

Questions and Answers on Effective Witnessing

If you are going to work with the upper-crust people—folks who are financially successful—you have to know how to deal with them. It doesn't make any difference to God if you have ten dollars or ten million dollars. He loves you just the same. But if you are going to work in a section of town where successful people live in their big homes, you have to approach them on their level.

Wear the best clothes you have. Get your hair fixed nice. Look sharp when you knock on that door. If you don't, you won't get anywhere. Remember that these people are financially successful already. If you don't know how to talk to them on their level, if you aren't dressed properly, you might as well forget it because they aren't going to listen to you. Unless you have a successful-looking appearance and manner, they will look upon you as ignorant, someone who doesn't know what he's doing or what he's talking about. They won't be interested in anything you have to say, even if you should manage to get into the house.

To witness to successful people, you have to appear successful. You must be dressed properly and fashionably. Your suit and tie must match. Your shoes must be polished. You have to speak clearly, confidently, and intelligently. The higher the class of people, the more important your appearance and manner become.

If you go out to witness in the slum areas of the city, what you wear isn't so important. Those people don't care if you wear a suit or a T-shirt and jeans. But if you are going to wear a T-shirt and jeans to witness, then go to the T-shirt district. There is nothing wrong with wearing T-shirts and jeans; but if you do, then go to the T-shirt part of town. To go anywhere else would be a waste of time.

You need to dress, speak, and act on the level of the people you'll be witnessing to.

Jimmy: Now when it comes to getting in the house, your appearance is important. In low to average income areas you must be friendly. I talk to those people like I've known them all my life. Then I just smile at them. I usually don't have any trouble at all getting in.

But in the higher income areas you have to be more reserved, a little more formal in your approach. "How do you do, Ma'am? My name is Mr. Maynor. This is Mr. Smith and Mrs. Jones. We are visiting from Such-and-Such Church. I wonder if we might come in and visit with you for a few minutes?" You can't be over-familiar with upper-crust people. You have to speak in a more refined manner or you'll never get in.

Always remember, approach people on their level, not yours. If you will do that, usually you won't have any trouble getting in.

Angelo: Also remember this: If three people of the same sex go together, make sure it's three women rather than three men. People are more receptive to a group of women than they are to a group of men.

Then when you knock on the door, remember to step back a little so it doesn't look like you are about to attack them. And smile! That may not be your nature, but do it anyway. You have to be friendly if you expect people to let you come into their homes.

When the person comes to the door, introduce yourself. Then introduce your partners. As you say, "This is Mary and Paul," they can step up a little bit. Be ready to be invited in, but don't get too close or seem pushy.

In some areas, the people may not open the screen door, but will talk to you through it. When this happens to me, I say, "I have something to give to you." I take along a tract or something so they have to open the door to accept it. Then when the door is opened, I walk closer to the person. Usually I don't hold a conversation through the screen door or through a crack in the door. I ask permission to come in. I say something like, "Ma'am, if you're not too busy, I'd like to come in and talk with you for a few minutes."

Most of the time people will let you come in. If they don't, don't get discouraged. Just go on to the next house.

Q. *What do you do if there is more than one person in the room to witness to?*

Angelo: That happens sometimes. You're going to run into situations like this. It happened to me not too long ago.

I usually begin by talking about the person's home. I don't go straight to the point. First I get friendly with the person. I say, "This is a lovely home," or other complimentary things to get their interest and attention. I might talk about their beautiful flowers or their fine-looking garden or the pictures of their children I see around the room.

This time I had two team members with me. We all sat down and I began to talk to the lady of the house. I had gone from my introductory remarks into my presentation of the Gospel. I had just gotten her to the place where I was going to ask her if she would like to accept the Lord Jesus as her Savior. I was about to ask her that question when two men walked in, her brother and a friend.

So, I made a friendly introduction. I said, "Come in, guys. We're having a little talk here, and I'd like you to be a part of it." So they came in and sat down.

I said, "I just asked your sister a question, and I'd like to ask you the same thing." So I went over again what I had presented up to that point. When I came to the place where I had left off with the lady, I asked all three of them the same question, "Would you all like to receive this gift of eternal life now?"

Then I said, "If you would like for Jesus Christ to be your Lord and Savior, I would like for you to pray this prayer with me."

Then I asked each one of them individually, "Would you like to receive Jesus as your Savior?" They all said yes, so I led them all in prayer.

When you talk to more than one person, make sure that everybody says yes, then lead them to the Lord—one message for all.

Questions and Answers on Effective Witnessing

Sometimes one will say yes, while the other says no. When that happens, you have to take the person who said yes into another room, or get right in front of his face and lead him to the Lord. Then go back to the one who said no. I never take the first no for an answer. I always go back and add another verse. When a person gives me an objection, I have the answer for it. Most of the time you can lead them to the Lord that way. Sometimes you can't. But I don't give up at the first no. I always give a person several chances to say yes to the Lord Jesus.

Jimmy: When you witness to one person, you want to sit by that person if at all possible. If you are speaking to a whole family, then you have to let them know that you're speaking to all of them. Talk to the entire family as if you were talking to one person.

I find that, as a rule, different people do different things. I tell them, "If it works for you, fine. Do whatever works for you."

When witnessing to a whole family, I try to lead the father to the Lord first. If I get him, I've got all of them, usually.

Not long ago I went to a home where there was a woman and her three daughters. I led the mother to the Lord, then the daughters followed her in accepting Jesus.

Angelo: You need to be extra careful in situations like that because if the mother objects, then you've lost them all. If she says yes, then you win them all. So you are going to have to pray. That's why you have the two team members there with you. While you witness, they pray.

Also, if there are little children around who might make noise and interrupt, your team members are there to take care of the kids, or the dog, or anything else that might interfere with you at that very important moment in those people's lives.

Jimmy: Once while I was witnessing to a mother, one of our team members took her two little children in the other room to play with them. One of the children was old enough to accept the Lord, so my teammate led him to the Lord.

You see, there is no set pattern. Each situation is different. Sometimes with a three-member team, one person can witness to mom and dad while another one takes the kids outside to play. (You should ask permission before you do this, of course.) That way one person can witness to the children apart.

Since there is no set way, you have to be led of the Spirit, because one set approach won't work every time you go out.

Angelo: But if you have an understanding of what to do in many different situations, then the Holy Spirit can prompt you as to which one will work in this particular case. You need to broaden your knowledge of how to handle people, even on a secular level. If you can find a good book about management, use it. Learn as much as you can about handling people.

Take the principles that people are using in the world and use them for the sake of God's kingdom.

Learn from them. Learn what works for them and apply it to the Kingdom.

Every situation can't be pinpointed, but you should learn as many things about handling people as you can. That way the Holy Spirit can prompt you as to which method or technique to use in any particular situation.

Jimmy: Again, it depends upon the age of the children. With smaller children, one person can take them and play with them to keep them entertained. With older children you may have to use a different approach. The main thing is to have someone with you to handle these things so you can be free to witness without interference.

Q. *Suppose you come upon a person who has been badly injured in an automobile accident. Should you lay hands on that person and pray for his healing? Should you try to witness to him in that situation?*

Angelo: In a case like that, I think you would need to pinpoint him. It's difficult to do, but you need to know about him before you can really deal with him. When you fall into a situation like that, you have to handle it on your faith and your faith alone. The person bothered with pain is preoccupied to say the least. He isn't going to be able to believe for himself.

If you don't feel that you are up to really doing something in the spiritual realm for him, don't try. Don't get over into laying hands on people, casting out devils, rebuking spirits, and all that kind of thing unless you really know you can do it. Otherwise, you will embarrass yourself and the Lord.

If you feel that your faith is at the place where you can do something about it, get in there and do it. You have to know yourself and know where you are. If you feel like you can do something to ease his pain while he is waiting for the ambulance, do it. If not, simply pray to yourself. You can pray in a soft voice to let him know that you care, that you are concerned, that you are wanting to do something to ease his pain until help does arrive.

Many times that is the best influence and the best witness you can have. He probably would be more influenced by that than if you jumped into the middle of the situation and started casting out demons. If you didn't know what you were doing and weren't up on your faith, you might do more harm than good.

Faith is something that you keep up. If you aren't at the place where you can do that person good, you are going to do him harm. A peaceful, quiet spirit will do more good about calming that person than anything else. Unless you are really going to take authority over the situation, don't do anything to call attention to yourself. Never act beyond your faith.

I've seen and heard of situations where people have happened upon someone like that and really did some good. But these people knew they could handle that situation. You see, you have to know about yourself. Sometimes you can best witness by being meek and quiet and doing everything you can to help that person ease the pain. That is the thing he is most concerned about at that moment anyway. Then later on you can talk to him about his spiritual needs.

Jimmy: You had better be careful about laying hands on people who have been in an accident because they could hold you liable. If you laid hands on a person whose back was broken, you might injure him permanently. Or you might open yourself up for a lawsuit.

In these cases, you have to be led of the Spirit. I have raised three people from the dead; but each time I had a foundation in my spirit to do it. You can't just go out and say words. Words don't get it done. You must have that foundation in your spirit and know that you can do it. Otherwise you are just making a wind and a noise. You would do much better just to pray.

You can bind up that pain without even touching the person. You can say, "Pain, I bind you, in the name of Jesus." You can start taking authority over the pain and asking God to help. But do it in a Christlike way. Remember, you are representing Christ. It makes me mad sometimes to see the way some Christians operate. They go out like wild men. They just don't have any sense. You have to remember that you are representing Christ. If you aren't careful how you act, you will turn people off instead of turning them on to Jesus.

Q. *Should you try to lead people to be baptized in the Holy Spirit when you witness to them about Jesus?*

Jimmy: No. Don't try to give them too much at one time. When you pull fruit off a tree, you can pull green apples as well as ripe ones. If you will wait until those apples are ripe, they will fall off the tree.

Don't get ahead of yourself. Don't try to get them into too much at one time. Get them saved and get them to studying on the new birth, their new life in Christ. Then after a week or two you can go back and visit with them about the baptism of the Holy Spirit. Make sure they understand the experience before you pray for them to receive the baptism. It is a beautiful experience, but they need to understand it.

Now the Holy Spirit will lead you in different ways. Not long ago I witnessed to a blind girl on the street. After I led her to the Lord, she brought her brother to me. Then I led him to the Lord, too.

He had already been baptized in the Holy Ghost, but had backslidden. He said, "Can you pray for me now that I can give my life back to God and be filled with the Holy Ghost?"

I said, "Yes."

I prayed for him and he began to speak in tongues. Then the Lord showed me through a word of knowledge that the girl wanted the same experience. I said to her, "Do you understand the baptism of the Holy Spirit?"

"Oh, yes," she said. "My family has experienced it. I've been to church and I know all about it."

I said, "Good. Do you want to receive it?"

Questions and Answers on Effective Witnessing

She said, "Yes."

When I laid hands on her, she began to speak in tongues. But this is not a pat thing. You have to be led of the Holy Spirit in each case.

Angelo: Sometimes people will want to get the Holy Ghost without any knowledge of what it's all about, even without being sure of their salvation. Make sure you explain the plan of salvation to them. Explain why they need to be saved and how to be saved. Then do exactly the same thing for the baptism of the Holy Ghost. Make it clear that these are two different experiences.

Suppose I stop a person and explain to him that he is a sinner, that he needs to repent and ask Christ to come into his heart. I go through the Scriptures with him. Then I ask, "Do you understand what you are going to have to do?"

He says, "Yes, I understand."

I say, "To receive eternal life, you have to repent of your sins and turn to Christ." I make sure that he fully understands the new birth.

That is one experience, but the baptism of the Holy Spirit is another. It must be explained just like the salvation experience. People need to understand that.

When you lead people to the Lord, you should go back and do the follow-up. Give them a tract or a little book about receiving the Holy Spirit. Say to them, "Now that you are saved, I would like to talk to you about another experience. Read this tract and

I'll come back again next week and talk to you about it." Don't get in a hurry. Give people time to fully understand what they are doing.

Jimmy: Follow-up work is very important. It's just as important as leading people to the Lord. You don't bring a baby into the world, then just dump it out on the sidewalk. If you do, you are defeating your purpose. You have to keep going back. Give those people literature to get them grounded in the Word. If you expect to lead someone to the Lord and keep him saved, you have to build a foundation in his spirit on the Scriptures. Step by step, you must get him grounded in the Word of God. Don't get in a big hurry. Take it one step at a time.

Q. *How do you know if a person is serious when he accepts the Lord?*

Jimmy: When I lead a person to the Lord, I ask if he really meant that prayer he prayed, was he really serious? Usually people will say yes.

When I am witnessing to someone, I don't know whether what I am saying is really taking root or not. So I ask, "Would you like to pray and ask the Lord Jesus to come into your life?" I lead him in the sinner's prayer. Then if I'm not sure he was serious, I just ask him if he really meant it. I get him to confirm his decision with his own mouth.

After that, you just have to trust the Lord. The full impact of that decision might not hit him right at that moment. But the next morning he might wake up and say, "Wow, I'm saved!" But you can't worry or wonder about people's sincerity. You just have to do your part by witnessing and leading them to the Lord, then leave the rest to God.

Q. *At what age can a child accept Jesus?*

Jimmy: When I was eight years old, I went to a revival. I was under conviction and wanted to be saved so bad that I could hardly stand it. I went up to the altar and told the people there that I wanted to get saved, but they said, "You're too young to get saved." It took eight more years for me to find Jesus. Eight years were wasted because that church turned me away.

Don't ever do that. Don't ever turn away a child who wants Jesus, regardless of his age.

Angelo: I have a tract that teaches how to lead little children to the Lord. It has pictures in it which explain or illustrate the plan of salvation to children so they can understand it. I have used it to lead little children about five or six years old to Jesus. All the Scripture verses the child needs to be saved are illustrated by pictures. Even though the child can't read, he can understand what you are talking about as you show the pictures to him. You can use this tract, and others like it which are available, to reach little children on their level of understanding.

Jimmy: Jesus said, *Suffer little children, and forbid them not, to come unto me: for of such is the kingdom of heaven* (Matt. 19:14). The important thing is to make sure the child understands what he is doing.

I have had people on my team who would go out just to see how many people they could lead to the

Lord. They were getting everybody they could to pray a prayer. They didn't even go through the Scriptures with them. They would come back bragging, "I led fifteen people to the Lord today!" Did they? No. Most of those fifteen people didn't even know what they were doing.

You must be sure that people understand what they are doing, regardless of their age. You have to explain it to them and get them to fully understand the decision they are making.

Q. *Is there any way you can lead a person to the Lord without using scriptures?*

Angelo: No, not really. It's impossible for us to lead people to the Lord unless we speak the Word to them. People don't get saved by our own ideas or beliefs, or even our experiences. They get saved by the Word. That is the only way.

The reason most people don't get saved is because they never get the seed inside them. So we have to do that for them. We have to get the Word of God to them. You can go out and testify of what the Lord has done for you, and that is good. But still the Word of God has to be planted as a seed in a person if you are to lead him to the Lord. Once the seed is planted inside him, then the Holy Spirit can bring it to his remembrance and convict him. The only way I can see that a person can get saved is through the Holy Spirit. There is no other way.

Jimmy: You might lead a person in a confession of faith without giving him Scripture verses, but he needs a scriptural basis of what has happened. It is only the Scriptures that will enable him to continue to stand. He may have enough understanding of the plan of salvation. He may realize that he is a sinner and that Jesus is the One Who came to save sinners. He might have a genuine experience and receive Christ as his Savior; but if you don't give him a scriptural foundation for what he has received, Satan can deceive him when you are gone.

Satan will come in and try to convince him that he didn't receive anything. But if you have given him a scriptural foundation, then he will have something to hold on to. If you have shown him from the Bible what has happened to him, then when Satan comes with doubt, he can say, "No, devil! I confessed Jesus Christ as my Lord and Savior, and the Word of God says in John 3:16 that whosoever believes in Him shall not perish but have everlasting life. I am saved because the Word of God says I am."

You see, people need a scriptural foundation for their beliefs. They need some tools in their hands, some definite scriptures to use to combat Satan. Otherwise they will begin to doubt whether anything really happened, especially if they are depending upon feelings.

That is why follow-up is so important—to see that a new-born Christian stands firm on his decision and is led to grow up into a mature Christian, grounded in the Word of God.

Norvel Hayes shares God's Word boldly and simply, with an enthusiasm that captures the heart of the hearer. He has learned through personal experience that God's Word can be effective in every area of life and that it will work for anyone who will believe it and apply it.

Norvel owns several businesses which function successfully despite the fact that he spends over half his time away from the office, ministering the Gospel throughout the country.

His obedience to God and his willingness to share his faith has taken him to a variety of places. He ministers in churches, seminars, conventions, colleges, prisons—anywhere the Spirit of God leads.

For a complete list of tapes and books
by Norvel Hayes, write:

Norvel Hayes
P. O. Box 1379
Cleveland, TN 37311

Feel free to include your prayer requests and comments when you write.

BOOKS BY NORVEL HAYES

You Can Be A Soulwinner

Jesus Taught Me to Cast Out Devils

Your Faith Can Heal You

God's Boot Camp

God's Power Through the Laying On of Hands

How To Protect Your Faith

7 Ways Jesus Heals

The Blessing of Obedience

Stand In The Gap For Your Children

How To Get Your Prayers Answered

What To Do For Healing

Holy Spirit Gift Series

Number One Way To Fight The Devil

Why You Should Speak In Tongues

Available at your local bookstore.

Harrison House
P. O. Box 35035 • Tulsa, OK 74153